Money Matters for Educators

A Guide to Budgeting, Debt, and
Retirement on a Teacher's Salary

Burke Wallace PhD, MBA

Disclaimer

This book is not intended to provide personal tax or financial advice. This information is intended to be used for information purposes only. The author is not an investment or tax advisor, and this should not be considered advice. It is important to do your own analysis before making any investment or employing any tax strategy. You should consider your own personal circumstances and speak with professional advisors before making any investment.

The information presented in this book is based on the author's own research and opinions. The information presented herein is believed to be true and accurate at the time of publication but does not guarantee the accuracy of every statement, nor guarantee that the information will not change in the future. No content from this book should be understood as constituting a recommendation to engage in any of the investment strategies presented.

ISBN-13: 979-8-9943588-0-1

Cover design by: Zirwa Anam

Dedication

To my parents, who have always wanted the best for me. And to Ryan, who is my daily reminder that life is about so much more than money.

Table of Contents

Wallace

Introduction: Why Money Matters

B eing an educator is, without a doubt, a noble profession. It is a calling, not just a job description. Those who choose to enter the field do so out of a desire to help people learn and, by extension, to make the world a better place. We all know the deal walking in: the intrinsic rewards help to make up for the lack of the financial ones.

Now, let's be clear: this book is not being written from some romantic, rose-colored-glasses point of view about what it means to be an educator. I have been around enough oppressive teachers' lounges, survived enough awkward staff Christmas parties, and sat through enough interminable mandatory staff meetings to know that our beliefs, temperaments, and opinions are as diverse, strong, and occasionally baffling as the rest of the country. Educators are not, as they say, a monolith. (If you are already internally rolling your eyes at the word *monolith* because you taught it last week in a vocab lesson, you should definitely thank a teacher, probably yourself, in the nearest mirror.) Yet, the core fact remains: no one chooses to teach because they want to become rich. We choose it to better the lives of our students and, let us be honest, all the glorious time off in the summer is not exactly bad either. It is the annual renewal cycle that keeps us coming back for another round.

The True Cost of Compassion

Need further proof that we are, at heart, an altruistic bunch? Just look at our spending habits. According to the National Center for Education Statistics, over 90% of teachers dipped into their own wallets to pay for school supplies. This is not just a few bucks here and there for a box of colored pencils. Based on their research, teachers are expected to spend over $500 on school supplies by the end of any given school year.

All told, that personal investment adds up to over $1.6 billion annually that teachers are collectively spending on supplies for their students. Think about that number for a second: a billion dollars, voluntarily spent, simply to ensure our students have the basic tools they need to succeed in our classrooms.

Now, let me put on my personal finance hat for a moment and give you an alternate scenario, a purely financial one, divorced from the necessity of keeping your classroom stocked. If you had invested that same $500 per year for a solid 10 years (that is a total of $5,000 invested, for those of you who hate teaching math and are already reaching for your calculators) and earned a conservative 6% return, you would end up with approximately $6,600 sitting in your investment account. That is around $1,600 of "free" money, generated by compounding stock market returns, that you are effectively missing out on every decade because of your compassion for your students. We must find a way to honor that generosity while also prioritizing your financial future.

This Book is Written for You

If you are reading this and you are an educator, whether you are in the classroom, the administration office, or even running a school library, I applaud you. Seriously. I wrote this book over many years, patiently shaping it and refining it, for educators like you. My goal is to help those who spend so much of their energy tending to the future of others to finally take charge and care for their own financial future. Of course, if you are not an educator, do not put the book down. The core principles of financial planning are universal and apply to all Americans, but this delivery system is uniquely tailored.

But why a personal finance book specifically for teachers? Do not all people need help with managing their money? Why yes, most certainly do. But this book is not for everyone, it is for you, and here is why educators need their own dedicated manual:

- **Unique Financial Circumstances and Retirement Plans:** Educators face financial challenges that are genuinely distinct from, say, a software engineer or a small business owner. We may have lower entry-level salaries and often have limited opportunities for rapid advancement in pay scale. Most importantly, we have complex state-specific retirement plans (pension, 403b, etc.) that operate under entirely different rules than the standard 401k plans most of the private sector uses. This book will provide tailored, relevant advice to help you navigate these specific challenges.

- **Educators are Critical Pillars of Society:** You play a role in shaping future generations that is unparalleled. Those energetic, sometimes frustrating, and often deeply underestimated creatures (the students you see every day) are one day going to be running our society. They will be the future CEOs, elected officials, and taxpayers. By helping you, the educator, to improve your financial literacy and security, we are helping you to better focus on your truly critical work without the constant, draining hum of financial stress in the background. A financially secure teacher is a more effective teacher. Period.

- **You are Automatic Role Models:** Hopefully, you are a role model both by virtue of the position you hold and by how you conduct yourself daily. But being a role model does not stop at the school building exit. By demonstrating responsible and successful financial practices in your own life, you can implicitly and explicitly inspire your students (and yes, your colleagues or teachers if you are an administrator) to become more financially responsible as well. Your financial health is a lesson plan unto itself.

So, what exactly makes this book different from the hundreds of other personal finance books available on the market?

To start, this book is written by someone who is first and foremost an educator. I have been exactly where you are, both as a professional navigating a public-school pay scale and as someone trying desperately to make that educator salary work for my family. I began teaching in 2004, and I have served in a variety of teaching and administrative roles in both public and private schools. I know the rhythm of the school year, the frustration of the annual contract negotiation, and the specific joy of a well-earned summer break.

My journey did not end there, though. After earning a Master's degree in Education with an emphasis in curriculum and instruction, my desire to better myself was not satisfied. As an adult I have always considered myself a life-long learner and still I feel that there is so much in the world I want to know about. That desire led me to pursue an MBA where I learned to better understand the financial side of education, and where I took a class specifically on personal financial planning. Over the years personal finance has become a passion of mine. Whereas some people listen to upbeat pop music during their workouts, I am that unique, slightly strange individual who happily listens to personal finance podcasts. My kids remind me often that this makes me extremely uncool. They are not wrong.

Bridging the Gap

Next, and this is crucial for accessibility, I have deliberately filled this book with examples and analogies pulled directly from the education profession. Just like you strive every day to scaffold new or difficult concepts for your students, I have worked hard to scaffold the personal finance concepts that intimidate many educators, making them understandable and relevant through real-world and classroom-based examples.

Think about it. Though the education field is brimming with intelligent people, people capable of explaining the nuances of the Common Core, the history of the Roman Empire, or the structure of DNA; there exists a surprising lack of financial know-how. Teachers must be incredibly well-rounded in their knowledge base. Elementary teachers are asked to be a master of all subjects necessary for success later in school, while secondary teachers get the small luxury of becoming a bit more specialized. Yet, for all but the STEM teachers, math often tends to be the subject many educators are least comfortable with. While financial literacy is (neglectfully, in my opinion) not one of the common core math standards, this foundational uncomfortability with the topic is a significant contributing factor to the avoidance of money concepts altogether. We avoid what makes us uncomfortable, and that avoidance costs us money.

The Financial Literacy Gap

This lack of financial literacy, to be fair, is not limited to our field. It is a national epidemic. Take a look at these sobering statistics from various recent surveys of American adults, conducted by various polling agencies, and see how many apply to you or your colleagues:

- **71%** say their monthly debt prevents building wealth.

- **43%** say they are focused on just surviving instead of improving financially.

- **32%** have no non-retirement savings.

- Over **25%** have no retirement savings.

- **40%** are not confident they will have enough money to retire.

- **42%** say finances negatively impact their mental health.

- **46%** of credit card holders carry credit card debt from month to month.

- **65%** grade their capacity to make good personal finance decisions as an A or B.

Unfortunately, the answers to wisely handling your money are not found in the teacher's edition of the textbook, and I guarantee your credential classes never prepared you for this absolutely vital aspect of your professional and personal life. We need a new textbook, and this is it.

Your Personal Finance Reading Strategy

What is the best reading advice you ever received as a teacher? For me, it was the power of choice, allowing students to read what they wanted so that they would organically develop their interest in reading. The classics will be much more palatable and meaningful to students if they first know the sheer joy of getting completely lost in a story that they chose. Standards can still be met while giving students flexibility in what they read, which is why, when I was an English teacher, my very first unit of the year was to allow my high school students to pick out their own book. There were many strict requirements, and I had to approve the book ahead of time, but they liked being able to choose what they read, and it was consistently one of the most successful units of the entire year.

What is the connection to *Money Matters for Educators?*

It is my sincere hope that by connecting the essential concepts in this book to the career you are already an expert in, that you will finally learn the joy of personal finance. It is not a chore; it is a form of professional development for your life. By mastering these concepts, you may finally experience the freedom that goes along with making the most out of your middle-class salary... a salary you earn through incredibly important, taxing, and valuable work.

So here is to you, educators. For those that already feel comfortable with your finances, you will find more than a few nuggets of wisdom you can use to improve upon what you are already doing and optimize your system. And if you are wondering why this all matters and think you would honestly rather be grading a stack of essays right now, please, read on! This is your permission slip. You can absolutely take care of your students and your future. Your money can work better for you than it is today. Your journey to financial confidence awaits!

REAL TEACHER TALK

I really should have started some sort of savings in year one, but back then my first contract was for $30,000 and I had a house, wife, daughter and a part time job so I don't know where the savings was going to come from.

- Mike (26 years as an educator)

My Story: An Educators Financial Journey

I first became interested in the concept of financial planning and, more broadly, being a good steward of my resources, during my college years. That initial spark was not a sudden epiphany; it was given as a gift. My dad handed me a book by financial guru Suze Orman, titled *The Money Book for the Young, Fabulous, & Broke.*

Now, let's be honest. Like most college students, the absolute last thing I wanted to do was read another book. I was already overwhelmed with required readings, research papers, and trying to sleep while my roommates played video games late into the night. But I was young and I was definitely broke. As for being fabulous, I figured two out of three was not bad, so I reluctantly started reading.

It did not take long for the topics in that book to excite me. It was like suddenly being handed the answer key to a complex test I did not even know I was taking. I realized there were concrete, measurable ways to use money, and that knowledge was empowering. That book started what has become a more than 20-year year interest, which ultimately inspired me to share what I have learned with my fellow educators.

Growing Up Middle Class

Over the years, I have spent a great deal of time reflecting on how my financial origin story has shaped my views on money as an adult.

Growing up, my family was solidly middle class. It was a classic American story, really. My dad was the first in his family to graduate from college. My mom was a nurse who later returned to school to get her bachelor's degree, also becoming the first in her family to do so. From an early age, they instilled in me the importance of education. It was not a question of if I would go to college, but where.

Both of my parents worked for most of my life. I spent many afternoons and summers in childcare and daycare, but my parents always made sure we were provided for. We lived primarily in working and middle-class neighborhoods, moving across the country from Pennsylvania, to Colorado, then Texas, and finally California.

Like many children, I did not think much about finances, and I do not think most students do. As kids, our financial understanding is limited to our immediate schools and neighborhoods. My first real awareness that extremely wealthy people existed, and just how lavish their lives could be, came from MTV's Cribs television show. I saw massive houses and luxury cars but I filed it away as "fantasy." Kids today, thanks to the proliferation of influencers and social media, have a far more immediate and often distorted view of wealth and inequality. It is right there in their pockets, amplified and filtered.

As a child, I did not have the latest and greatest things, but my needs were always met, and then some. When most of my friends had the new Nintendo 64, I was still grinding away on a Sega. When the cool kids wore expensive Nike shoes, I showed up in BK Knights. But here is the key realization: I was not really aware of the kids wearing hand-me-downs, and I certainly did not know that free or reduced lunch programs existed. That kind of financial blindness is a hallmark of a comfortable, middle-class upbringing. We often do not see the struggles right next to us because we are not struggling ourselves.

There were, however, periods when one of my parents was unemployed. As a child, that did not register much in terms of bills or finances. What I did feel was the frequent moving that came with job changes. Living in multiple states taught me adaptability and how to make new friends. Since this is a story about my financial upbringing, the lasting lesson was learning the importance of hard work and providing for your family, no matter where life takes you.

My Financial Education: The First Paychecks

I did not receive a regular allowance as a kid nor did I get everything I asked for. My first real-world, cold-hard-cash lessons came with my first job in high school. Because my parents strongly emphasized education and because we were financially stable, I did not have to work during the school year. Instead, I worked during the summer, built up a savings cushion, and then quit once football season started.

My first official job, as a slightly awkward sixteen-year-old, was at Hollywood Video. Yes, I am now old enough to have had a first job in a field that no longer exists. Hollywood Video was not as widespread as Blockbuster Video, but we were the place where customers experienced the red-carpet treatment. Our stores were designed to resemble a Hollywood premiere, complete with acne-ridden teenagers dressed in cummerbunds and bowties, helping customers find the latest VHS release. I probably said "Be kind, please rewind" as many times as I have told students to "Be quiet" throughout my career.

This minimum wage job taught me a crucial and somewhat painful life lesson: how quickly a paycheck can disappear. I would trade time with friends to work, receive my paycheck, deposit it, and then, within a few days, watch my bank account decrease. I quickly realized that if I did not intentionally decide where my money went, it would disappear more quickly than I wanted. That early realization became the foundation for my later understanding of the importance of budgeting. I did save some of those early paychecks, too. I do not remember having a detailed plan for my savings other than knowing I would need it throughout the school year. Looking back, this was my very first, rudimentary emergency fund.

The Uncool Car

My parents also helped me by purchasing my first car: a 10-year-old Pontiac Parisienne. Seriously, look it up. It had a heavy, boxy, old-man aesthetic. I can attest to just how uncool it was for a sixteen-year-old to be driving. But it was a car of my very own, and I could fit a boatload of friends on the front and back bench seats. That thing was a tank.

A few months into driving, I got rear-ended. The impact ruined the front end of the other person's brand-new car. The only damage to mine was a pushed in metal bumper. My dad and I promptly popped it back out with a rubber mallet. That experience taught me the value of durability and function over flash and status. That car became a meaningful symbol of my developing financial understanding of needs versus wants.

Frugality in College

My young adult life was marked mostly by privilege and good fortune, and I fully acknowledge that. Without the support of my parents, or the basic health to work, I could have ended up in a very different position. In college, I was able to choose jobs based on my enjoyment or to learn skills to help me in my future career, rather than out of necessity to pay tuition. I attended a small, private college in Southern California, and had the student loans to prove it.

My jobs varied widely. I worked as a student assistant in the School of Education, which gave me my first taste of the administrative side of school life. I also coached football for a local high school that had just won the state championship, and I served as a youth group director at my church. During my first few summers at home, I even worked at a local Mexican restaurant. Sadly, I did not discover the joy of guacamole until after my time at the restaurant ended. Otherwise, I could have had my fill using my 50% food discount. Enjoying the work you do is, in itself, a privilege that not everyone has the opportunity to experience.

If I had to describe my financial life in college, I would use the word frugal. I mostly stayed on campus and enjoyed the many free and fun activities that were offered. Being more of an introvert, I preferred a weekend sitting in a friend's dorm room talking and hanging out, rather than heading into Los Angeles to go clubbing or to some trendy, overpriced restaurant. When I did go out, I always read the menu from right to left, meaning I looked at the price first, before deciding what I would order. That simple habit became an early, unconscious budgetary control mechanism. Thankfully, I never developed a taste for alcohol, which has saved me a significant amount of money over the years. I shopped for clothes on the clearance rack and loved the end of the school year when I could hunt through the piles of perfectly good items my fellow college students discarded as they moved out. Free stuff!

A Hard Lesson

I graduated a semester early, which saved a lot of money, but soon afterward, I lost my first job as a college graduate. Looking back, that experience has shaped nearly every financial decision I have made since. It was a horrible, sinking feeling to wonder how I would pay my bills.

The panic was real. As a new college graduate, my ego was tied into proving I could make it as an adult, even though I knew I could move home if necessary (which I eventually did years later). That moment of professional and financial instability became my greatest learning experience. Since that day, I have worked to maintain a robust emergency fund in my bank account. I treat it like a well-structured lesson plan that I hope I never have to teach.

But if I ever lose a job again, or for some reason cannot work, I will have money to pay my bills for a solid period of time. That safety net is invaluable.

Thanks to my connections, I had an affordable room to rent in a house with a group of other guys, and I soon landed a job at a restaurant. The better money, however, came from catering weddings and bar mitzvahs on the weekends, which I did whenever I could. Catering became my financial side-hustle, a critical tool for educators who want to increase their income without relying solely on step increases. All the while, I was in grad school working toward my master's degree, which kept me busy and gave me a good excuse not to spend a lot of money on entertainment. I would eat at my job or cook simple meals, making leftovers last a couple of days.

Entering the Classroom

After a few years in the restaurant, which reminded me again that the service industry is not for the faint of heart, my roommate got a job at a local private school. He mentioned they needed another teacher and encouraged me to apply. The rest, as they say, is history. My first few years of teaching, without ever having taken an educator preparation class, were a whirlwind of barely controlled chaos. They were also a solid step up in my income. I coached football after school and continued catering on the weekends. Each of these side-gigs I genuinely enjoyed, had time for, and substantially increased my income without leading to burnout.

That first year of teaching was when I discovered the magical world of employer-sponsored retirement savings. As a private school, there was no state pension, but they did offer a 403b retirement plan. I signed up and contributed 6% of my paycheck because the school would match 50% of employee contributions, up to 6%. I later learned it would take years of employment for the school to reach that full 50% match. In my first year, the employer match was some small amount, about 1% of my pay. But I reasoned that if I started contributing 6% on day one, then I would not miss it going forward, and eventually the employer match would grow. Even with my first full-time job, I knew that getting an employer match on retirement contributions is free money. I am not one to pass up free money, especially when all it takes is setting aside some of my own salary to receive that additional money from the school.

Big Guy in a Little Car

Coinciding with this my full-time job came the inevitable need to buy my first car without parental support. I had managed to keep the car my parents purchased for me in high school in good working condition, but eventually, the engine developed problems that were simply too costly to ignore. So I "adulted" as they say, and went car shopping on my own.

From my personal finance studies, I knew that getting a car lease is almost never a wise financial move, but I was genuinely nervous about taking on debt while already struggling to pay my monthly bills and student loans on a private school teacher salary. Vehicles are one of the largest purchases most people make, and I did not want to make a mistake. So I approached the process like a research paper: I researched the cheapest, most reliable cars from every manufacturer, test-drove the ones with the best ratings, and ultimately purchased a Hyundai Accent.

If you have ever seen the classic SNL skit of Chris Farley singing "fat man in a little coat," that is exactly how I felt driving it. Big guy in a little car. But it was a sound financial decision. It met my transportation needs, I purchased it entirely on my own, and wisely, I paid it off within 24 months.

Private to Public

After four years working in private schools, I realized that education was a field I could see myself in for the long term. This realization led me to the next phase of adulthood: going back to school to earn my teaching credential so I could secure a job in a public school and finally earn a living wage for my work.

This is where the power of family support truly became a blessing. Living back at home provided immense financial relief, allowing me to pay off all my remaining student loans and cover my credential classes one at a time, with cash. This temporary sacrifice of moving back home was the key that unlocked my future financial security.

Despite completing my teaching credential during the depths of the Great Recession, I eventually found a job. It took two grueling years of hiring cycles, temporary positions, and periods of unemployment, but I finally entered public education. This was a critical step not only to earn more money but also to gain access to decent benefits and begin contributing to the public teacher's pension system.

My First Home: The Power of Prudent Spending

I was fortunate to live with my parents for a few years, which allowed me to become more financially stable and save for my first home. My relationship with my parents is wonderful, and I am extremely grateful for that time. While living with my mom, she did not charge me rent. After paying bills and saving each month for a house down payment, I devoted the rest of my money to paying off my student loans. Eventually, I paid off my own loans and the Parent-PLUS loan my mom had taken out to bridge the financial gap during my private college education. She took out that loan out of love, wanting the best for me, but I did not feel right saddling her with debt, especially after all she sacrificed to put me through school. Paying it off was a huge weight lifted.

Living with my dad had a few more strings attached, in the best way possible. He also did not charge me rent, as long as I contributed to my retirement. That was a pretty sweet deal, and one I may replicate if my own kids live at home as adults. I am forever thankful for his wisdom about the importance of saving for retirement early. During that time, I opened a Roth IRA and began contributing to it regularly.

I bought my first house in 2009. It was a modest 2-bedroom, 1.5-bath condo in a blue-collar town, and I was incredibly fortunate to purchase it near the bottom of the Great Recession housing market. I put 20% down, a decision I strongly recommend to avoid Private Mortgage Insurance (PMI). The purchase price was about 1.5 times my annual salary, which was manageable but, unfortunately, almost unheard of today in most parts of the country. After some initial renovations and adjusting to all the monthly expenses of homeownership, I realized I could comfortably maintain my frugal lifestyle. I put any left over money toward my mortgage each month, essentially doubling my payments, and paid off my condo in just three years.

By my early thirties, I was a homeowner and completely debt free. It was an incredible feeling of safety and security, knowing that if I lost my job, I would still have a place to live. Since I maintained an emergency fund, I knew I would be okay financially for at least a short while, no matter what came my way financially. Being debt free has become a core strategy for my family's security and peace of mind.

There was some luck involved with that housing market, but it was not just luck. I could have purchased a much nicer home in a fancier neighborhood but I was not married and did not have kids yet, so a highly-rated school system was not important to me. Choosing affordability and function over prestige and status helped set the stage for my long-term financial comfort. Since a home is usually a person's largest lifetime expenditure, housing decisions have a far greater impact on future financial stability than almost any other spending decision.

Starting a Family

In my late 20s, I got married. This is a crucial point, arguably more important than buying a house, because who you marry has the biggest single influence on your financial future. I had read many times that finances can be a major source of tension in relationships. The conversations we had about potentially spending a lifetime together included deeply honest discussions about money alongside the more typical relationship considerations. It has always been important to me to be with someone compatible across the many facets of life and partnership.

I do not want to make our relationship sound like a business transaction or cold and distant, it is not at all. But this is a finance book, not a relationship book, and getting married shaped my financial future, as it does for everyone. We were financially aligned, meaning we both prioritized saving, avoided debt, and lived below our means.

Shortly after our wedding, which was an intimate and beautiful event that did not break the bank, we moved for my spouse to start grad school. We were able to rent out our condo, which provided a small, steady stream of additional income on top of my teaching salary while my spouse worked only a few hours a week. The condo purchase truly kept on giving. Because I had been committed to saving and living below our means, we had accumulated enough money to pay for grad school with cash, while using our earnings to cover living expenses.

It was during my 30s that I discovered the wonderful world of thrift stores. I found them before Macklemore's *Thrift Shop* song became popular but still far too late in life! I could have been scoring deals for years, yet for some reason, I never considered thrifting. Maybe it was because we were living in the Bay Area of California for grad school, surrounded by some of the coolest thrift stores I had ever seen, filled with reasonably priced treasures. Suddenly, shopping was not a financial drain; it became a fun, frugal treasure hunt.

The Trade-Off of Conservative Choices

We eventually moved back to our condo to begin the process of growing our family through adoption. Thanks to some fortunate timing and my network, I was able to return to my previous public school. Because of valuable work experiences I gained while my spouse was in grad school, and encouragement from mentors who recognized abilities in me that I had not yet seen in myself, I quickly advanced into administration, which significantly increased my income.

After the adoption was finalized, we sold our condo, which had become tight with a child running around, for over double what I had paid. I was ecstatic. However, there is an important lesson for the reader. Although this was great news, making more than double the low purchase price from eight years earlier resulted in a smaller total amount of money than friends who purchased more expensive single-family homes. They did not double their purchase price when they sold, yet they earned a higher total dollar amount of appreciation than I did. In this case, my extremely conservative approach to finances actually limited the money I could have earned by purchasing a more expensive home initially. It is the constant balance between safety and optimized return.

Still, selling the condo gave us a solid down payment for our first single-family home in our new town. Despite the higher purchase price, we were able to keep our monthly mortgage payment reasonable thanks to the down payment. Like with my first home, we lived below our means, and with my spouse working a full-time job and my administrative role, we were once again able to pay off our home in just a few years.

Building My Nest Egg

This is also the period in my life, my late 30s, when I finally became serious about saving for retirement. Thanks to my parents' insistence, I started putting money aside with my very first full-time teaching job at a private school. Though the employer match was minimal, I still started those payroll deductions because everyone has to start somewhere.

A few years into teaching, I learned about the many benefits of the Roth IRA (discussed more fully in a later chapter). Anyone whose income is low enough to qualify can open one on their own, independent of an employer. I opened a Roth IRA and set a goal of maxing it out each year. At the time, the maximum contribution was $5,000, which worked out to just over $400 a month, so I made it a non-negotiable part of my monthly budget.

When I moved from private to public school, I stopped contributing to my school-sponsored retirement account because California required nearly 10% of my earnings to go toward the state teacher pension system. However, I never stopped contributing to my Roth IRA. From those early years onward, regardless of my job, I have maxed out my contributions every year. By my late 30s, I began increasing the amounts my spouse was saving in 403b and Roth IRA accounts, and started contributing to my own 403b through my school, on top of the pension and Roth IRA contributions.

The first decade of my investments saw little growth, due to the small amounts I had invested and living through the Great Recession. In the second decade our investment nest egg grew considerably. This growth was partly due to the overall rise of the stock market, but it was primarily the result of the undeniable power of compounding. Compounding is the ability of your money (in this case, your investments) to generate earnings not only on the amounts you contribute but also on the interest and growth accumulated over time. It is like a curriculum that continuously builds on itself until you look back and realize you have created a mountain of expertise.

Tracking Net Worth

I began tracking my net worth at the age of 37. Before that, I had never really considered it. Having any "net worth" worth tracking seemed like something only older people did. Retirement felt far away, and though I was always saving, I was also focused on enjoying the present. Despite all my reading, I found few authors who discussed the importance of a net worth statement. Since I started tracking it yearly, I have found it to be the single most valuable summative assessment to determine how my financial life is progressing (or regressing). It has become so important that I include more information on the topic in the chapter on budgeting.

Even after all these years I still look forward to the end of December. Not just for the long-awaited winter break, but because I get to calculate our net worth for the year and update my tracking spreadsheet.

My net worth is calculated fairly simply:

1. I start by determining our house value minus any mortgage debt. To estimate the house value, I consult a few online sources and take a conservative average of the results.

2. Next, I add the Kelly Blue Book trade-in value of our cars, any cash in our bank accounts, all our investment accounts, and the cash value of my pension. I include the pension's lump-sum cash value because it provides a tangible yet conservative estimate of a benefit that many people overlook.

3. If we have any debts, which we try to avoid, then I subtract those.

I became a net worth millionaire at age 40, largely due to the rapid rise in California home prices. I emphasize "net worth millionaire" because it differs from being an asset millionaire. Some consider only cash and investment assets as defining a true millionaire. We reached the asset millionaire milestone when I was 44 which includes my spouse's assets. As I mentioned earlier, getting married has the single biggest impact on your financial future. On my own, I would not yet qualify as an asset millionaire.

Your net worth is not a straight line. Moving from California to the Midwest temporarily reduced our net worth due to housing prices and the costs of fixing up our new house, which are not immediately reflected in home's value. Additionally, as our net worth grows, investments naturally make up a larger share, which exposes it to stock market fluctuations. Overall, our trend is upward, though some years have seen temporary decreases.

Mistakes Help Us Grow

As the T-shirt my kids' school gave to all students one year as part of their PBIS (Positive Behavioral Interventions and Supports) program stated: "Mistakes help us grow". I have made plenty of financial mistakes along the way. Finances are not separate from the rest of our lives, and sometimes I made decisions for reasons other than money that were not necessarily the best financially.

That is okay. The key is recognizing the mistake and learning the lesson.

Below I use the term "mistake" lightly but here are some non-financially optimal "mistakes" I have made along the way that I hope you can learn from:

Mistake 1: Savings Priority

When we adopted our first child, he was seven. We were thrilled, and part of our desire to provide him with the best life possible included preparing for his educational future. We pulled a significant amount from our savings and put it into a 529 college savings plan. In theory, this was a good step, but most financial experts agree that parents need to prioritize saving for themselves first. There are no student loans for retirement. We postponed investing for several years to catch up on what we thought we should save for our child's future college as "good parents". The hard financial lesson we learned is that we could have maximized our own retirement savings first, secured our future, and then focused on the kids' college fund. By doing otherwise, we lost valuable years of compounding due to misplaced priorities. More on this concept is in the Investment chapter.

Mistake 2: Ignoring Investment Fees

My first investment account outside of my work retirement plan was a Roth IRA, which I opened at the local credit union where I was a member. I had opened an account there a few years earlier because they offered a better rate on a car loan for my first self-purchased car. I did not know much about investing other than the principle that you should put money away, so I trusted the financial advisor at the bank. She placed me into funds that were very expensive. The funds performed adequately, but they had a high expense ratio and a delayed sales charge that took additional fees out for the first five years I owned the funds. They were so costly that I eventually sold them, but not before losing money on returns due to the drag of those fees. From this experience I learned the valuable lesson that a low fee (expense ratio) is one of the single most important factors in successful long-term investing.

Mistake 3: The Cost of Immediate Enjoyment

My spouse and I really enjoy being at home. We like to go out and explore the world, but most of the time, sitting quietly at home with a movie or good book, or spending time with family, is what truly rejuvenates us. Because of this, when we buy a house, we tend to invest a lot of money renovating it into a home *we* will enjoy. I have never understood why so many people fix up a house right before selling it. Financially I know why, but we have always wanted to enjoy our home and make improvements while we are living in it.

So far, we have lived in each home for less than a decade. While home prices in California appreciated fast enough that our early renovations paid off when we sold, I learned the hard way that home prices in the Midwest do not rise as quickly. We put far more into our Wisconsin home than we got back when we sold it. We moved earlier than expected, and although the price did increase, it did not cover the cost of all of our renovations. Even so, the move from Wisconsin, while causing a financial hit, was possible because of our strong financial standing. This allowed us to take advantage of an unexpected opportunity to move to Montana to be closer to family.

Mistake 4: Over-Aversion to Debt

I am pretty cautious when it comes to finances, as you have seen throughout this chapter. This approach has been safe, and I have avoided much financial stress and worry as an adult, which is a priceless benefit. However, it has not been the most optimized path to maximizing financial return. Much of my adult life has focused on getting out of debt and staying out of debt. I have never had a car loan or a mortgage over 7%, yet the S&P 500, the 500 largest stocks trading in the U.S., has returned an average of almost 12% over the last 50 years.

Paying off my house early saved me the interest I would have paid, but my money could have earned much more had I invested it instead. This is called opportunity cost. If I had not been so averse to debt, I might have ended up with a larger nest egg. While this is a financial mistake of sorts, it is one I do not regret, because the priceless comfort of being debt-free has brought peace to me and my family.

Mistake 5: Moving

My 40s are not over yet and we have already moved across the country... twice. Neither of these moves was for my job. The first move happened in the midst of finishing my PhD dissertation but, as they say, life is an adventure. Moving from California, where I had worked my way up to a senior administrative position, to Wisconsin, I took a job with teacher-level pay at a small school, even though the position combined teaching and administrative duties. This represented a significant pay cut. A few years later we moved from Wisconsin to Montana, this time to be closer to family. Once again, I took a pay cut from what I was earning in Wisconsin to become a professor of education at one of the Universities in Montana.

The 40s are generally considered peak earning years. Instead I took two pay cuts and definitely felt the impact on our financial life. Money is not the goal in life, it is only a tool to help us enjoy the time we have. These moves were not made for financial reasons. Still, from a purely financial perspective, they were not wise decisions and the consequences will have long term impacts on my financial life. Fortunately, these moves would have been much more difficult if we had not already built a strong financial foundation. As Benjamin Franklin once said "By failing to prepare, you are preparing to fail."

Believe It, Achieve It

Financially speaking, that brings us to the present day. We have grown our family, moved homes, continued to spend less than we earn, and continued to save toward retirement. Each year has brought slightly different circumstances, but I am at the point in life where my financial habits have solidified and have served my family well.

I have worked on this book on and off for over a decade. Reflecting on my life when I first started this book, I am more mature now but also more tired. My three kids take most of the energy and brain capacity I once devoted to working side-gigs. And I am now at the age where different parts of my body are starting to randomly ache. If I can clearly see how I have slowed down just over this last decade, then I can only imagine how ready I will be to retire when the time comes.

Thankfully, I can see a point in the future where we will have enough money saved that, thanks to the continued power of compounding, it will grow into our target amount by our desired retirement age. At that point, we can strategically slow down on investing and redirect those dollars to enjoyment in the present. Perhaps we can even reduce our work commitments to something lower stress or part-time. We have positioned ourselves financially so that we do not anticipate needing to work all the way to 70 or even to full Social Security age. Through our investments, my educator pension, and Social Security (in whatever form it may take when I retire), we will have enough for a comfortable financial lifestyle starting in our early 60s.

Of course, life is unpredictable, and there are lots of curveballs I may face. Including the ultimate reality that none of us are promised tomorrow. Recently my spouse was diagnosed with a serious health condition. As anyone who has received such a diagnosis knows, it changes the trajectory of life. But this does not mean we should stop planning and working to make tomorrow all we want it to be. Our tomorrow may now focus more on healthcare than vacations but it is still a future worth working toward.

This is my financial story so far, and I want to help you reach a place where you can look forward to your own tomorrow, confident in your financial security. It is possible. Read on to find out how.

Wallace

Believe it, Achieve it: Financial Mindset

A s a football coach, I created a team motto each year. It served as a rallying cry to unify the players around a common theme. One of my favorites went like this: when all the players gathered in a circle, hands held high together, the team captain would yell "Believe it!" and the team would respond "Achieve it!" Then the captain would yell "Achieve it!" and the team would respond "Believe it!"

These themes are not meant to withstand rigorous logical scrutiny. This is not a philosophy dissertation. Yet they are profoundly effective. They are designed to help a group of hormonal teenagers focus on the bigger picture and, most importantly, connect their internal belief to their external actions.

As you begin reading this book, this is a fitting theme for you as well. You must believe that you can live a better, more financially secure life in the future in order to achieve it. This is not just fluffy motivation; it is the fundamental principle of your financial growth mindset.

The Educator's Goal-Setting Playbook

In a sense, every educator begins a new school year with this exact motto in mind. You must believe you will accomplish the learning goals during the year in order to eventually achieve them. You must believe that reaching the end of the year will result in a measurable, positive outcome for your students.

I am not talking about counting down the days until summer break, although we have all done that at least once. If you have ever taught seniors, they may write the remaining days of school on the whiteboard, but little do they know that teachers are often just as excited for the final bell!

I am referring to starting the year with a clear set of goals, a scope and sequence of what you hope to achieve. If you are a classroom teacher, you know precisely what students need to learn by the end of the year. If you have had the good fortune of teaching the same class or subject for a while, you may even know what benchmarks need to be met each semester or month. You do not just walk in and wing it. You plan. You assess. You adjust. Your financial life deserves the same dedication.

Administrators undertake similar exhaustive planning. They believe in creating a better educational system and spend much of the summer planning professional development, hiring the right staff, upgrading buildings, and refining policies to make the year run more smoothly. When I was an administrator, I always started the year by asking: What do I want to have achieved by the end of the year? What should my teachers know so they are fully equipped? How does the school culture need to evolve? What new policies from the legislature need implementation? Sometimes we had to pivot and adjust our goals, a mid-year curriculum adjustment of sorts, but it was crucial to never lose sight of why we were doing it: for the students.

The same principle applies to your financial life. You must envision where you realistically want to be, believe you can get there, and then work to achieve that belief. In the short term, where do you want to be at the end of each month before your next paycheck? In the long term, where do you want to be the day after you turn off the lights in your classroom or office for the last time? How do you want to live your life now and in retirement? How do you want to spend your most precious gift, the gift of time?

How you manage money can either empower you or profoundly hinder your ability to achieve these goals.

REAL TEACHER TALK

I'm saving as much as possible perhaps to work less once I get past the 25 years-of-service mark for my pension.

- Kelsey (15 years as an educator)

Your financial IEP

Author and inspirational speaker Simon Sinek encourages people to start with their "why." Your why comes from your deepest beliefs and purpose. While his book focuses on organizational leaders discovering the why for their organization, the principle also applies directly and critically to your personal finance journey.

Think of your why as the foundation from which you can begin scaffolding additional knowledge and learning about your financial life. Why do you need to manage your money better? Why is it important to prioritize your spending and saving? Why are you planning for the future now, when retirement may feel far away?

Before you can fully embrace the ideas in this book and make them work for you, you must first identify your financial why and then develop a financial Individualized Education Plan (IEP). What specific goals must your money meet for you? Is it financial freedom? Providing for your family? Or simply eliminating the anxiety of living paycheck to paycheck?

Once you know what you want for the present and the future, you can begin developing measurable and attainable goals for your financial IEP. Understanding your goals and believing in their importance provides the foundation for making wise decisions about your money. When you know why you are tracking your budget, investing your money, or practicing delayed gratification by living below your means, you are on the fast track to financial responsibility. Financial professionals often call this goals-based investing, and studies consistently show that individuals who commit to a clear financial plan are far more likely to stick with it through market ups and downs.

The Three Phases of Retirement

As you begin to envision what your future life could be like, remember that not every year in retirement will be the same. Is every school year identical for you? Do the classroom management techniques that work one year always work the next? Of course not. Retirement is similar. Consider the phases of life as a long-term financial curriculum map to guide your planning.

Financial experts often recommend planning for a 30-year retirement. If you retire when you first qualify for your pension (usually sometime in your 50s) or when your pension age factor maxes out (usually sometime in your 60s), then you do not have to be a math teacher to realize a 30-year retirement puts you into your 80s or 90s. With the average lifespan in the U.S. in the late 70s, a 30-year retirement could very well be your reality. Planning for longevity is essential.

Retirement can be broadly divided into three phases, which I like to think of as three distinct curricular cycles:

1. The Go-Go Phase

This phase, often called the golden years, usually begins right after retirement. Your health is still strong, you have energy, your mind is sharp, and you can enjoy a lot of activities with your newfound freedom. This is the first day of summer break feeling that lasts for years. When people imagine retirement, they often picture the Go-Go years.

- **Activities:** You may want to travel the world or visit family frequently. Have you dreamed of a cruise or an RV trip across the country? Do you want to volunteer your time, or finally sleep in and spend a leisurely lunch not worrying about the bell ushering you back to class?

- **Spending:** Spending is often high during this phase because you have more time and energy for enjoyable, often costly activities.

Some retirees work part-time during the Go-Go phase just to stay active. As a retired educator, you may have opportunities to work as a substitute teacher, earning extra income while choosing your schedule, grade levels, and schools. Of course, many retired educators have no interest in returning to school once they retire. There are many opportunities, but to make the most of your Go-Go years, it is essential to plan for these expenses.

REAL TEACHER TALK

I intend to live a full retirement with plenty of travel and a comfortable income. I contribute 15 percent of my income to retirement. Also, I intend to leave an inheritance to my children.

- Elaine (15 years as an educator)

---

2. The Slow-Go Phase

Next comes the Slow-Go phase. In this stage you are getting older and life begins to slow down. You must become more selective about how you spend your time because your body can no longer "Go-Go" all the time.

- **Activities:** This phase can still be very fulfilling if you are financially stable. You may focus on nurturing local relationships and taking advantage of community events. If you are fortunate enough to live near a university, it may offer a 50-and-better program with activities and mentally enriching lectures. Otherwise, nearly every community provides social and physical opportunities designed for seniors.

- **Spending:** Spending typically declines during the Slow-Go years as you are less likely to take as many expensive international trips and instead find enjoyment in simpler, less physically demanding parts of life.

3. The No-Go Phase

Finally, if you are fortunate to live long enough, you will reach the No-Go phase. During this period, your pace slows even further and will be limited by your ability to be mobile. Most people take the ability to get around for granted, but as the body ages, that independence is no longer guaranteed. Mental decline may also occur during this phase, though take solace that you may not be fully aware of it!

- **Activities:** Social connections may diminish, and the ability to live independently will become a major consideration.

- **Spending:** Spending during this stage varies widely but is largely focused on basic living expenses and, most importantly, healthcare. If you need to move into a retirement community or assisted living facility, costs can rise rapidly, making this phase especially expensive. Your No-Go phase is absolutely not the time to run out of money.

Behavioral Finance

Your ultimate success in managing your money, whether you are a substitute teacher or the superintendent of the largest district in your state, comes down to your behaviors and your mindset. That is why this book begins with the end in mind. In academia and the investment industry, this concept is known as behavioral finance.

Behavioral finance is the study of how our humanness influences financial decision-making. You are human, even though some consider educators superhuman, and there are things in life that matter deeply to you. It is important to understand what those things are, because they influence how you manage your money and how you live your life.

However, you also have biases. All of us carry deeply ingrained beliefs about money, taxes, saving, spending, and retirement. These beliefs are shaped by our families of origin, our culture, and our past experiences. These biases are similar to the student who believes they cannot do math because an older sibling struggled. Just as we teach that student to overcome the belief, we must also teach ourselves how to overcome our own biases.

Below are a few common biases and how they may affect both your
teaching life and your financial life:

Financi al Bias	Definition	Teaching Analogy	Financial Impact
Status Quo Bias	The preference for keeping things the way they are, avoiding change.	Sticking with the same lesson plan or teacher's edition textbook you have used for 15 years, even if it is outdated.	Failing to switch from high-fee retirement accounts to low-fee funds because the paperwork is intimidating.
Present Bias	Prioritizing immediate rewards over future ones.	Procrastinating grading a stack of essays until the very last moment, despite knowing the future stress it will cause.	Delaying starting your retirement savings plan, costing you thousands in future compounded growth.
Herd Mental ity	Following the crowd to feel safer or avoid regret.	All the teachers in the lounge decide to buy a lottery ticket together, even though the probability of winning is minuscule.	Chasing the "hot" stock your colleague mentioned at the staff meeting, rather than sticking to a diversified, long-term plan.

As you work toward achieving what you believe your retirement
should look like, and as you read through the information in this
book, it is important to identify your personal financial biases.

Examine your spending habits and pinpoint areas where you tend to overspend. Understanding these patterns is the first step toward creating a more realistic and sustainable budget.

If your current approach is not producing the results you want, then something needs to change. This book offers suggestions, but no suggestion will be effective unless you are willing and able to do it. Follow through with it. Take time to consider any lifestyle changes that may affect your financial situation.

Think carefully about what matters most to you and how you want to allocate your resources. Consider what will be important to your future self. Your financial habits should align with your priorities and values.

EXTRA CREDIT: Find an app or website that lets you upload a photo of yourself and conducts age progression on your photo. A recent study showed when people picture themselves in an elderly state, they are significantly more likely to save more for retirement. Seeing those wrinkles and gray hair (or lack of hair in my case!) will help you face the reality that your body is ageing and someday you will not be able to work. This simple exercise helps break through the present bias and connects you emotionally to your future self, making saving feel less like a sacrifice and more like an act of love for that older you.

Time is the Treasure

Ultimately, money is a tool, not the end goal.

The greatest resource each of us has is time. We trade this precious time to earn money so we can provide for our basic needs and many of our wants. Beginning with the end in mind requires sacrifice. You will have to give up some things now, perhaps a few immediate pleasures, to benefit your future life. You may need to give up more time to work more or give up certain pleasures to reduce your spending. But do not do this simply to accumulate more money. Do it to reclaim your time.

To paraphrase the words of Jesus, "What good does it do a person to gain the whole world but lose their own soul?" Career success and the amount of money you have are not the root of all happiness. There are plenty of wealthy people who are profoundly unhappy. However, money supports happiness because it gives us control over aspects of our lives. Money is a means to an end.

With financial savviness, you can enjoy the present, do the meaningful work of educating children, and prepare for a future where you have the financial flexibility to live entirely on your own terms. You can always earn more money but you can never earn more time.

The choices you make today dictate your future. This principle applies to health, relationships, and life, and in this book. It is the reason you keep reading. This is not a professional development training you are forced to sit through. You are here because you have only one life, and you want to take care of yourself financially now so you can live the life you want later.

Believe it. Achieve it.

Wallace

Budgeting: Your Financial Formative Assessment

Budgeting is about as sexy as sitting through the annual assessment data, yet without it, you do not really know how you are doing or where you can realistically improve. Think about it. If your budget is nothing more than checking your bank account balance at the end of the month, that is no better a measure of your financial health than only looking at a student's final grade at the end of a term.

Sure, if you have more money left at the end of the month than you did last month, you are technically "passing the class", but how can you know which areas are your true strengths or persistent weaknesses? Just like a final grade, your bank balance is only a summative assessment. It tells you what happened, not why it happened or how to change the outcome next time. Yes, there is always anecdotal evidence (such as thinking you ate out too much); however, anyone who has been through an intense accreditation process at their school knows that only gets you so far.

Accreditors want evidence, and financially speaking, so should you.

The good news is that educators love a good free template. In the appendix, this book provides a sample budget worksheet that you can use as a starting point to build your own. Even better, no single budgeting method works for everyone so you are free to adapt one that works for you.

I once interviewed for an instructional coach position and was asked what the best 5th grade math curriculum was. I knew immediately that was not the right school for me. No single curriculum is the best fit for all students, just as no single professional development model can solve every challenge a school faces. In the same way there is no perfect budgeting method for everyone. What matters most is finding a system that works for you. Finding a system that works, even if it is imperfect and requires adjustments, is better than not trying at all.

A Budgeting Picture

Do you actively keep any type of budget? If not, you might think you are in the minority, but you are not alone. As I have tracked survey trends over my decade of working on this book, the results have been remarkably consistent. Over 75% of Americans claim they have a budget of some kind. And yet well over half of American adults admit they do not follow a budget, even if they technically have one, or they follow it only "in their heads." Imagine if we kept our grade books only in our heads. The principal would have a fit. Furthermore, Gallup and other pollsters have found that only about one third of American adults keep a detailed and consistent budget. These numbers tell us that the majority of Americans engage in some form of rudimentary, often mental, budgeting, though it is likely not as detailed or effective as it could be.

Let us start with the basics. We are going all the way back to elementary school math addition and subtraction. When you add up all your monthly expenses and subtract them from your monthly income, the result matters. If you are spending more than you are making, you are in trouble. Despite the poor example set by our federal government, spending beyond our means is not sustainable. Unfortunately, unlike the government, we cannot just print our own money. Eventually deficit spending will catch up with you.

If you do not find yourself in this situation, kudos to you. You are already ahead of the curve. If you do, there are only two ways to fix it. First, you can **spend less.** Second, you can **earn more.**

For many years, I coached, supervised after-school activities, or taught summer school to earn extra money and make ends meet. No one ever said personal finance was rocket science. It is simple math combined with hard work.

This reality highlights a deeper problem. A college friend of mine is a teacher in Arizona, a state historically known for limited government support for educators. She recently posted a photo on social media of her celebrating an award she had received. However, it was not a "Teacher of the Year" award. It was an "Employee of the Quarter" award from the restaurant where she has worked nearly full-time for the past several years. I was shocked, though I should not have been. A person so passionate about helping her students has been forced to work long hours each week as a waitress just to afford a comfortable middle-class lifestyle as a single woman. That is not right.

This book is written for her, and for so many of you like her. Reading it will not change public policy overnight; however, if it helps your dollars work a little more efficiently, allowing you to work a little less or enjoy retirement a little more, then the time you spend reading will be unequivocally worth it.

But I digress. Let us return to the nuts and bolts of how to make those financial goals happen.

Different Types of Budgeting

Let us look at a couple of different ways to keep a budget.

1. The Line Item Budget

When you think of a typical budget, this is probably the type that comes to mind. It is also the most helpful for beginners and experienced budgeters alike because of its versatility.

With this approach, you create a list of the major spending areas in your life. How detailed you make it is entirely up to you. The budget can be as simple or as complex as fits your lifestyle and your commitment to financial responsibility. I have seen some line-item budgets that are as detailed as a guidance document issued by the federal Department of Education, in other words, painfully detailed.

Your line item budget should be as detailed as you find both helpful and realistic to follow. I do not recommend having too few lines, as that can lead to overspending within broad categories. For example, in the sample line item budget found in the appendix, you will notice several shopping categories. Shopping for household items is separated from shopping for clothes. When all shopping or entertainment expenses are grouped together, results become less accurate and it becomes easier to overspend within a specific category without realizing it.

If you allocate $300 for "shopping," and consistently exceed that amount, it becomes difficult to identify the source of the problem.

Are you overspending on clothes or are you purchasing more classroom supplies than expected?

This is the same reason our grading software allows multiple categories within a gradebook. Greater detail helps students understand how a specific assignment affects the overall outcome of their grade, which in this case represents your budget. It also clarifies what steps are needed to improve that outcome. On the other hand, if you prefer the freedom and flexibility of broader categories, you can try that approach and evaluate how well it works for you. Budgeting is about finding a system that fits your habits while helping you track spending and stay within the limits you set, ultimately supporting long-term financial stability.

This budgeting method works best in a spreadsheet where you can easily add or adjust rows and columns as your needs change. Finding the right template online can be almost as exciting as discovering the perfect free lesson plan. There are also paid digital tools like YNAB (You Need A Budget) or Monarch Money. I generally prefer not to pay for something I can do for free, but budgeting is a challenge for you, the cost of an app may be worthwhile.

2. The Envelope Budget

This method of budgeting takes a lot of work, but it can be a powerful and tangible way to get your spending under control.

With more and more of our financial transactions happening digitally, this approach to budgeting may feel a bit old-fashioned. I include it because, just like with our students, a hands-on, and tactile approach sometimes works best. If you have a hard time saying no to sale items or those small impulse purchases near the checkout line, you may want to consider this method. It does not have to be permanent, but it can be helpful for a season.

In this method, you still need to develop key spending categories and determine how much cash each category can support. Once those categories are established, you withdraw cash from your bank account at the beginning of each month and place the appropriate amount of cash into labeled envelopes. Every time you spend money from a category, you pay for it in cash and remove that amount from the correct envelope. The strength of this budgeting method is simple. Once the cash in an envelope is gone, you literally cannot spend any more in that category for the rest of that month. You can not spend what is not there.

But what about that great sale you saw advertised online? You could still make the purchase, but you would need to take the cash from one of your other envelopes. The question becomes whether you are willing to give up spending in one category to overspend in another. That choice is completely acceptable and there is no need to be hard on yourself for making it. The key principle of this budgeting method is learning to recognize and manage trade-offs.

This idea of trade-offs is so important that I used to give my students "oops passes" each semester. If a student forgot an item for class or needed to use the restroom, they turned in one of their oops passes. At the end of the semester, any unused passes could be redeemed for extra credit. It was both amusing and surprising how quickly students decided they could wait rather than leave the room when an unnecessary bathroom trip came at the cost of extra credit. Each of those moments became a small but meaningful lesson in trade-offs.

If an all cash system feels impractical, a hybrid approach may work better. You can use envelopes only for discretionary spending. Discretionary spending includes expenses that vary from month to month and represent luxuries rather than necessities. Categories such as entertainment, dining out, clothing, technology, and general shopping fall into this group. And yes, fellow educators, alcohol is not a necessity, even when little Tommy in the back row makes you want a drink before lunchtime.

3. Un-Budgeting Budgeting

Some financial experts argue that you do not really need a detailed budget as long as you pay for your obligations first. I use the term obligations loosely here, since contributions to savings or retirement accounts are not technically required. However, they are essential if you hope to achieve financial independence.

Although I personally use a line-item budget approach, I still prioritize paying my obligations first. When my paycheck arrives, I immediately pay my mortgage and utility bills, donate to charity, transfer money to my high-yield savings account, and contribute to my Roth IRA. These are my financial priorities and they must be paid before anything else. Supporters of this approach believe that as long as you do not spend more than you earn, any money left after meeting your obligations, including saving for retirement and the future, can be spent however you choose.

If you have the self-control and discipline to stay within your earnings for the month and still reach the end of the month having covered everything you need, then this approach may work well for you. It may also appeal to those teachers with messy desks who prefer flexibility and do not like being confined by the structure of a strict budget. Think of this method as unschooling for budgets.

Solving the Problem

Budgeting is like Common Core math standards for the primary grades. It involves adding and subtracting numbers to make sure the final result stays above zero. Regardless of the budgeting method you choose to use, the ultimate goal is the same, to track your income and spending so you consistently spend less than you earn.

The concept really is that simple, although for many people, putting it into practice is far more difficult than understanding it. So what do you do if you grasp the concept but still cannot balance your budget? The good news is that you have three options. You can spend less, you can earn more, or you can do both.

REAL TEACHER TALK

Budgeting is a team effort with my husband. We both work hard to make it all come together for our family. We work off a solid budget and try to plan for emergencies. It also means we have to prioritize spending and make sacrifices.

- Heather (21 years as an educator)

Option #1: Spending Less

Spending less can be surprisingly difficult in our consumer-driven society. We live in a service economy where there is never a shortage of new, shiny objects to buy. In fact, much of the U.S. economy relies on people spending on money they do not need. Still, if you want to lower your spending, you can. I have yet to meet an educator who finds it impossible to reduce their monthly expenses.

When looking for ways to reduce spending, start with the largest items in your budget and work your way down. This is sometimes called targeting the "Big Three" expenses, because they consume the largest portion of the average American's paycheck.

- **Housing:** Most people spend the largest portion of their income on housing. The best way to reduce expenses here is to purchase a home or find a lease within your means. I enjoy watching HGTV but often get frustrated when a couple is shown a dwelling that is above their budget. Of course that house or apartment is going to be nicer. It is rare for a couple to resist the temptation of a more luxurious dwelling and stay within their budget.

- **Transportation:** The same principle applies to the vehicle you drive. Leasing a vehicle is one of the worst financial decisions you can make. With a lease, you make continual payments without ever owning the vehicle. Vehicles are depreciating assets, meaning they lose value over time, unlike houses, which can gain value. If you purchase a vehicle, you will eventually own it outright. The average lease payment in the U.S. now sits around $600 per month. Swapping a $600 monthly lease for a reliable, modest vehicle you own outright frees up $7,200 a year for savings.

Even if you do not lease, your vehicle loan payment should not exceed 10% of your gross income. To reduce spending, opt for a quality, affordable car rather than one that might impress your students. If possible, consider walking, biking, carpooling, or taking public transit. These options save money on gas, reduce wear and tear on your car, improve your health, and are better for the environment.

- **Food:** Your food budget is highly flexible. Treat your food consumption like a class period and meal planning as your lesson plan. By knowing exactly what you will "teach" (cook) each day, you minimize impulse purchases, reduce food waste, and avoid last-minute takeout orders. Many generic brands offer the same taste and quality as name brands but at less cost.

Option #2: Earning More

If you cannot make your budget work through spending cuts alone, another option is to increase your income. This might involve moving to a different district, transitioning into administration if you are a teacher, or advancing into a higher administration position if you are already an administrator. As a professor of Education in Montana, I have observed that many of my students hope to find jobs at one of the nearby Native American reservations, where schools often offer higher pay than nonreservation schools. Additionally, some of the districts along Montana's borders with neighboring states struggle to attract and retain teachers because crossing state lines can result in significantly higher salaries.

REAL TEACHER TALK

I transitioned from teaching to administration so my wife could stay home with our children.

- Dan (26 years as an educator)

Barring the big career changes mentioned above, for most educators looking to increase their income, it likely means taking on a side hustle. One of the biggest perks of teaching is the schedule, which offers long breaks and consistent, manageable hours during the school day. In a recent year, I added over 25% to my base salary through side hustles, all while maintaining a good work-life balance, avoiding burnout, and still having time for family and leisure.

Through your current employment, you can take on athletic coaching duties, or earn extra income from additional supervision responsibilities such as Saturday school or summer school. Early in my career, when I was at the bottom of the salary schedule and single, I coached and signed up for every extra duty I could find.

The good news is that there are countless opportunities for teachers to earn side income in the evenings and summers. As a content expert you could tutor. With experience in curriculum and understanding student needs you could write and sell your own lesson plans online. You could teach a course or run a summer camp. If you have a master's degree you could do as I have done for so many years and take on an adjunct professor position. Alternatively, like my Arizona friend, you could work in the service industry which provides a completely different experience and a break from education.

There is an opportunity for everyone if you need and want it, but it comes with a trade-off: time away from family and friends. Time is our most precious resource, which we never get back, so consider your choices carefully.

It is also important to know that a side hustle can be temporary. It does not have to be permanent. A former colleague would set a specific income goal each year from driving passengers around. Once he reached the goal, which he used to fund his summer vacation, he stopped his driving for the rest of the year. Another teacher taught summer school the year her daughter was getting married but did not continue the following year. Side hustles can be temporary solutions for specific, measurable goals.

Option #3: Do Both

Most of you who are serious about balancing your budget will likely end up doing both: cutting expenses in some areas and finding ways to earn a little extra. You get an A+ from me as long as you make it work.

REAL TEACHER TALK

It feels like a shell game sometimes, especially now that I am on a single income. In the teaching profession it is challenging for people to make ends meet on the salary especially with the higher cost of living. I work as much overtime as possible to help offset my current salary.

- Melissa (13 years as an educator)

Budget Percentages: Differentiated Instruction for Your Wallet

Budgets are personal. This is not the time for a prefabricated test that comes with the textbook. While I provide a sample budget worksheet, you must adjust it to fit your own needs. Just as you are the teacher and you should tailor a test to what you actually taught, your budget should also be adjusted based on your individual circumstances.

However, as a general guideline, your financial differentiated instruction, the following percentages can serve as a starting point if you are unsure of where to begin. These percentages are based on your take-home pay (net income), which we will define below:

Category	Recommended Percentage of Take-Home Pay	Breakdown
Housing	25-35%	Rent/mortgage, property tax, utilities, insurance, maintenance.
Transportation	10-15%	Loan payment, gas, maintenance, insurance, public transit.
Food	10-15%	Groceries, eating out, coffee, alcohol.
Debt Repayment	10-20%	Student loans, car loans, credit card debt (above minimums).

Savings/ Investing	10-20%	Retirement investments, emergency fund contributions, long-term savings. **While the numbers in this chart are for net income, your goal should be to put 20% of your gross income towards retirement.
Entertainme nt/Misc.	5-10%	Hobbies, shopping, subscriptions, personal care.

If you prefer a simpler approach, which I do not necessarily recommend for long-term optimization but that offers more flexibility, the 50/30/20 method is popular:

- 50% of your take-home pay goes to Needs (housing, basic transportation, essential groceries, minimum debt payments, insurance).

- 30% of your take-home pay goes to Wants (entertainment, clothes, travel, dining out, subscriptions).

- 20% of your take-home pay goes to Savings and Debt Payoff (investments, emergency fund, saving for a down payment, or paying off debt *above* the minimum).

Gross vs. Net Income

Notice I often say "take-home pay". This is also known as your net income, which is the amount you receive after all withholdings are deducted. The salary you earn on paper is your gross income. No one actually takes home their gross income.

Think of it this way: gross income is like the total class roster before anyone drops or is absent, while net income represents the number of students who are actually in the room and ready to work.

Taxes, union dues, pension contributions, insurance premiums, and any investment deferrals such as 403b or HSA contributions are deducted from your gross income, leaving you with your take home pay amount. If you are allocating a significant portion of your paycheck each month to a retirement account like a 403b or 401k, your take-home pay will decrease. This may make your budget feel tighter, but it is not a loss, you are simply investing that money into your future self.

The Emergency Fund

For as long as I have been interested in personal finance, research has consistently shown that a large number of Americans are financially fragile. Since 2014, Bankrate.com has conducted an annual nationally representative poll on Americans' ability to handle an unexpected $1,000 emergency. Year after year roughly 60% of respondents reported that they could not manage a $1,000 emergency.

Where do you fall on that bell curve? Perhaps you are young and healthy and think emergencies will not affect you. But emergencies are not limited to health issues: your car could break down, you could get pink slipped, or if you own a home, an appliance might fail. Unexpected expenses are always possible.

How do students pass a pop quiz? By being prepared. How do you survive a financial emergency? By being prepared with a money cushion known as your emergency fund.

Occasionally, when teaching a college course, a student would ask what they needed to do to pass. You might be wondering the same thing about your emergency fund: how much should you save? Both are good questions because they address the heart of preparedness.

The standard recommendation is to save three to six months of expenses saved in your emergency fund. Not three to six months of salary and not three to six months of what you think you should spend, but three to six months of actual, documented expenses. That is why budgeting is step one.

I am naturally fiscally conservative, so I try to keep more than six months of expenses in my emergency fund. My family has built up to this level over the years. In general, three to six months is sufficient because if you lose your job, or cannot work due to illness or injury, you should immediately cut back on all non-essential spending. This ensures the normal three to six-month fund can last even longer.

As an educator, unless something truly unexpected occurs, which, again, is the purpose of an emergency fund, your job transitions should ideally align with the school year. This timing offers greater predictability than for most workers, but the safety net remains essential.

Net Worth

Once you have a budget that you are actively tracking, the next logical step is to track your net worth. Your net worth is a simple equation. The good news is that you do not need a math teaching license to figure it out. I am talking about multi-step elementary-level math here.

Net worth is the single most important report card of your overall financial health because it measures the cumulative effectiveness of your habits over time.

To get started, add up all your assets. Assets are things you own that have economic value. Examples of assets to include in your net worth calculation are property (such as homes), vehicles, cash in bank accounts, investments, retirement accounts (including the cash-out value of your pension), etc.

Next, subtract any liabilities you have. Liabilities are financial obligations or debts. Common liabilities include mortgages, vehicle loans, student loans, credit card debt, etc.

The amount you have left is your net worth.

Total Assets - Total Liabilities = Net Worth

That is it. This is simply a multi-step addition and subtraction word problem. Tracking this number every year, and comparing it to previous years, is the truest measure of your progress toward financial freedom.

EXTRA CREDIT: Calculate your report card by creating a net worth statement. You can search online for a free spreadsheet that will do the math for you. Look at sample net worth statements to see the various types that are out there and find one that works for you. Make this an annual appointment (perhaps every December, as I do) to check your progress.

Wallace

Debt and Credit: Borrowing with Purpose

W hen I was taking classes toward my Master's in Business Administration, I was shocked to learn just how much debt is the engine that drives our economic growth. Have you ever really thought about that? Most of us probably understand that an individual goes into debt when they borrow money to purchase something they cannot otherwise afford. Student loans are a prime, and often necessary, example. If you are like the average, college-educated American, you took out loans to help pay for your bachelor's degree. You borrowed money from the bank, which you eventually paid back or will pay back. The bank charges interest on the loan so that you end up paying more than the original amount borrowed. In turn, the student loan money goes directly to your college or university, enabling you to take classes.

That is Debt 101. But let us aim for greater mastery of the idea, from a macroeconomic perspective. What did your college or university do with those tuition dollars? Most of it went to paying their staff and a portion probably went to servicing loans for campus buildings.

Here is where debt starts driving our entire economy, like a massive, interconnected school district. In addition to enabling you to attend college now instead of tutoring kids for ten years until you saved enough to pay cash for your college degree, the borrowed money pays the salaries of your professor and the lunch lady. Debt expands the economy. The professor uses their salary to buy groceries for their family and likely to pay the monthly mortgage debt on their house. The grocery store uses that income to pay their clerks and to purchase more inventory. That purchase provides income to the truck drivers that got the food there and the farmers who grew the food. The truck drivers who delivered the food and to the farmers who grew it. The truck driver and farmers in turn use that money to pay for braces for their child. The orthodontist, in turn, uses that money to grow their business and cover personal expenses.

Do you see the point? Debt is necessary for economic growth because it allows transactions to happen now instead of forcing everyone to wait years until they have the cash to fund them.

But this is not a book for your 12th-grade AP Economics class. This is a book for teachers and other educators, designed to help you master your personal financial life. While debt can be beneficial at the societal level, is it good at the personal level? The answer is both no and yes. In our society, unless you are a trust fund baby, debt is mostly unavoidable while you are young and building wealth. If you manage your money wisely, debt is not something you need to remain in permanently.

Good Debt vs. Bad Debt

Not all borrowing is equal, and not all debt is bad. Think of debt like school assignments: some build your long-term knowledge and career potential, while others are just busy work that disappears the minute the bell rings.

Good Debt is debt that has the potential to increase your net worth or help you meet your financial goals. This is debt used to purchase an appreciating asset: one that generally gains value over time.

- **Mortgage Debt:** Because housing prices tend to increase over the long term, mortgage debt is generally considered good. If you are a teacher and own a home, it is likely the biggest purchase you have ever made and may someday represent a large portion of your net worth. As the value of your home rises, so does your net worth.

- **Student Loan Debt:** Earning a higher education degree opens up opportunities to increase your future earnings and therefore your net worth through additional job opportunities, higher salary schedule steps, or administrative roles. My decision to return to school for my teaching credential and master's degree opened up doors in the public school system and directly increased my lifetime earnings. This investment in your human capital is considered good debt. That said, you should not borrow recklessly. It is still important to limit debt and plan for how you will repay it in the future.

If good debt helps you meet financial goals or increase your net worth, what is bad debt?

Bad debt is anything that hinders your financial situation in the long term or is used to purchase a depreciating asset: an asset that loses value rapidly over time.

- **Credit Card Debt:** This is the worst offender. It becomes bad debt when you purchase non-essential items that you cannot afford to pay off at the end of the month. According to the Federal Reserve, the average interest rate on credit card accounts assessed interest currently hovers around 22%.

- **Vehicle Loans:** By this definition, vehicle loans are technically bad debt because a car loses value the moment you drive it off the lot. But you might be thinking, "I need to get to school on time." Of course, you do. What I am suggesting is that when you look for your next vehicle, consider the long-term financial impact of taking out a large loan and instead choose something affordable and reliable. It is okay if that old adage about the cars in the student parking lot being nicer than those in the staff parking lot rings true. Limiting bad debt will help you achieve long-term financial success.

As a general rule, the interest rate you pay corresponds to the type of debt. Good debt tends to be cheaper to borrow than bad debt. Generally, the interest rate on a mortgage is lower than the interest rate on a car loan, which is almost always much lower than the interest on an unpaid credit card balance.

Paying Off Debt

If you find yourself with debt and want to pay it off so that you can use your salary for more exciting purposes, you have options. Think of it like a student with a low grade who is desperate to improve before the end of the term. That student must study to raise their grade, and you must live within your means so that any extra money you have can go towards paying off your debt.

The two main philosophies for paying off debt are the rational approach and the emotional approach. As with most things in personal finance, the approach that works best depends on what will be most effective for you. Personal finance is not a factory production model of education where one size fits all.

The Rational Approach: Maximizing Efficiency

The rational approach is known as the "Avalanche Method." This method is mathematically sound and focuses on efficiency.

1. List all your debts from highest interest rate to lowest interest rate.

2. Continue to pay the minimum payment on all debts.

3. Put all extra money toward the debt with the highest interest rate.

4. Once that debt is paid off, you add the entire amount you were paying (minimum plus extra) to the minimum payment of the next highest interest rate debt, thereby building an avalanche of debt payoff.

The reasoning behind this approach is purely financial: the higher the interest rate, the more you pay in interest on the loan. Being the resourceful educator you are, why pay any more money to a bank than necessary? This method can save you the most money.

Money Matters for Educators

The Emotional Approach: Maximizing Motivation

Alternatively, the emotional approach is known as the "Debt Snowball." This method is rooted in socioemotional learning and behavioral psychology.

1. List all your debts from the smallest balance to the largest balance.

2. Continue to pay the minimum payment on all debts.

3. Put any extra money toward the debt with the smallest total balance.

4. Once that debt is paid off, you take all the money you were paying toward that debt and add it to the minimum payment you are making on the next smallest debt. This creates a snowball effect where more and more money goes toward your debts as you pay each one off, giving you small, immediate victories that keep you motivated.

While this method may cost you slightly more in interest over the long run because you are not prioritizing the highest-interest debt, the psychological benefit of eliminating a debt completely can be the spark many people need to stick with a long and challenging payoff journey. It is the difference between assigning one massive term paper (Avalanche) versus providing several smaller quizzes (Snowball) to keep engagement high.

Loan Forgiveness for Public Service

As of the writing of this book, educators working in certain school settings may qualify for forgiveness of part of their federal student loans. The two main programs are Public Service Loan Forgiveness (PSLF) and Teacher Loan Forgiveness (TLF). These programs are primarily for those working in public service; however, private school educators working for non-profit schools may also qualify. Eligibility depends on the length of time you teach and the type of school where you work. Loan forgiveness amounts vary by program

These programs exist at the discretion of the federal government, so we will not dive deeply into the specifics. I trust that as a molder of young minds, you can research the current federal policies when you read this book. Start with the official government source:

www.studentaid.gov

These are federal loan forgiveness programs, so the steps may be complex, and the paperwork can be confusing. Yet the effort to determine eligibility and pursue forgiveness is worth it. Even if it takes you a full 40 hours to read, understand, and apply and let us say $10,000 in loans are forgiven, it would still be worthwhile. Even $5,000 in forgiveness is valuable. No educator I know earns $10,000 for a week of work.

Consider the time spent versus the financial benefit: this process may offer one of the best return on investment (ROI) opportunities for your time. Think about how many after-school clubs you would need to supervise or sports you would need to coach to earn the equivalent of your forgiven loans. In this sense, the loan forgiveness paperwork could be your highest-paid side hustle.

If you are new to education or early in your career, take the time now to understand what it takes to have your loans forgiven. The outcome could have a significantly positive impact on your financial future.

Until your loans are forgiven, stay on top of them. Make your monthly payments. If you are struggling, review the chapter on budgeting. Remember this key idea: to make your budget work, you must either spend less or earn more. Any debt, even good debt like paying for an education that leads to a fulfilling job can hold you back from achieving financial independence and the freedom to make your time your own.

Credit Score

Any discussion about debt would be incomplete without looking closely at your credit score, which is a three-digit number that tells lenders how trustworthy you are. Think of it as your financial report card or GPA. It summarizes your history as a borrower and dictates the terms, including interest rates, on your next major loan. A higher score earns you the best financial "scholarships," meaning the lowest interest rates on mortgages and car loans.

Keeping your financial transcript in good shape is critical. A difference of just 100 points on your credit score can mean the difference between paying $30,000 or $50,000 in interest over the life of a single 30-year mortgage. How many months would you have to work to earn that much money, only to lose it to bad habits? Stay on top of your payments, use credit responsibly, and make sure your financial transcript earns you that A+.

More on this in the next chapter.

Credit Score: Your Financial Transcript

I n modern American society, it is extremely hard to avoid the world of credit. I will not say it is impossible, because some people do live off the financial grid, so to speak. Towards the end of my years living in California, almost every summer brought devastating wildfires. One, the Camp Fire of 2018, destroyed entire mountain towns. A couple of my staff members tragically lost their homes in that blaze. I remember reading a news article about a year later stating that the government faced challenges providing some of the fire victims with financial restitution because those individuals had no financial life recorded in any system. They had to open up bank accounts and establish credit just to receive some of the payments that were being offered.

This extreme case is a powerful reminder that whether you like it or not, participating in the modern economy means engaging with credit. Absent a truly catastrophic event, each of us has a credit score that determines our creditworthiness. Whether you know it or not, your creditworthiness as measured by your credit score impacts multiple, often non-obvious areas of your life.

Your Financial Report Card

You need to understand how to use credit because every one of us has a credit report, which results in a credit score. Do you know what is in your credit report? Do you know your score?

Think of your credit report as your official financial transcript, detailing every course (loan) you have ever taken and the grades (payment history) you received. Your credit score is the resulting Grade Point Average (GPA).

This score is a three-digit number that represents an individual's creditworthiness, based on their credit history. It is used by lenders and financial institutions to assess the risk of lending money or extending credit to a particular person. The most commonly used credit scoring model in the United States is the FICO score, which ranges from 300 to 850, with higher scores indicating better creditworthiness. A high score can increase your chances of being approved for loans or credit cards with favorable terms and lower interest rates, while a low score may result in higher interest rates, stricter borrowing requirements, or even denial of credit.

FICO Factor	Weight	Description
Payment History	35%	Have you paid every loan and credit card bill on time? This is the most important factor.
Amounts Owed	30%	How much credit are you using versus how much you have available (your credit utilization ratio)? Keep this below 30%, ideally below 10%.
Length of Credit History	15%	How long have your accounts been open? Older accounts help your score.
New Credit	10%	How many new credit accounts have you opened recently? Too many looks desperate and lowers your score temporarily.
Credit Mix	10%	Do you have a healthy mix of different types of debt, like credit cards, installment loans (car/student), and mortgage?

You are entitled to one free credit report per year from each of the three major credit bureaus: Experian, Equifax, and TransUnion. If you find an error, you can contest it with the credit bureau, just as a student should challenge a mistake on their transcript. Studies show that up to one in five consumers have a report error that negatively impacts their score, making it critical to check your report regularly. As you will see below, maintaining an accurate credit score and striving to improve it can pay significant dividends.

In recent years, many credit card companies and banks have also started providing their customers with a monthly credit score. While this is not as thorough as a full credit report, it gives users a quick snapshot of their financial standing. If you want to check for errors, you will need to obtain one of the free annual credit reports.

The Cost of a Low "GPA"

The larger the purchase and the longer the term of the loan, the greater the effect a small change in your credit scores can have on your interest rate. This is where your financial GPA either earns you an interest rate scholarship or sticks you with crippling costs.

For illustration purposes, consider a $250,000 mortgage on a house with a 30-year term.

Interest Rate (Due to Credit Score)	Total Interest Paid Over 30 Years	Difference from 4.5% Rate
3.5% (Excellent Score)	$154,140	Saves $51,876

4.5% (Good Score)	$206,016	Baseline
5.5% (Average Score)	$261,010	Costs $54,994 More

Source: Bankrate Loan Calculator

As you can see, the interest rate you pay, which is partially determined by your credit score, can have a significant financial impact on your long-term wealth. In the high-interest scenario, the borrower may end up paying more in interest than the original $250,000 loan. That extra money, over $106,000 compared to the best rate, is the salary you earned and time you traded, simply gone in interest payments.

A car loan, which is smaller and shorter in term, will result in less variation in total interest paid. However, financially savvy educators should avoid paying more than necessary for anything. Improve your credit score and you will pay less in interest.

The Wide-Ranging Impact of Your Credit Score

Your credit score influences many aspects of your financial life beyond mortgage rates, credit card interest rates, and loan approvals. Essentially, your credit score is your financial reputation, and it follows you everywhere.

- **Insurance Rates:** Your credit score can affect your insurance premiums. Statistics show that people with lower credit scores file more claims, so insurance companies often consider it when setting rates for car and home insurance.

- **Renting:** Landlords and property managers may also use your credit score to decide whether to rent to you or not. A high score indicates that you are a reliable, low-risk tenant who honors commitments.

- **Utilities and Cell Phone Service:** If your credit score is low, you may be required to pay large deposits for utility hookups such as electricity or water or for a cell phone contract.

Generally, the higher your credit score, generally the more likely you are to qualify for insurance, secure better rates, and rent a desirable apartment or home without paying extra fees. Hopefully this illustrates that your credit score has far-reaching effects, it is the price of admission for accessing the best deals in modern society.

EXTRA CREDIT: Set calendar reminders every four months to check your credit score at one of the credit bureaus (ex: January check Experian, May check Equifax, and September check TransUnion). By spreading out your credit report review over the year, you will be more apt to catch an error early rather than letting it fester like a missing assignment, and drag down your score.

What is Credit Good for Anyways?

Credit lets you borrow money you do not have. How many credit cards do you own? Do you know your approved spending limits on them? Do you pay off your credit cards each month? These are important questions to frame the discussion.

Credit card use is acceptable but from a financial perspective, carrying credit card debt is worse than failing to input attendance for the entire year and then trying to back-log everything from your paper attendance sheet into the student information system. At least with attendance, someone from the office will be there to remind you. With credit card debt, the high interest rates just continue to compound and grow, and there is no administrator to bail you out. That interest is money spent on items you have already consumed, hindering your ability to pay for new necessities.

Consider the preceding paragraphs my "first week of school" approach to credit: I am being firm in my classroom management and expectations so that the rest of the year goes more smoothly. In reality, credit and credit cards can be a beneficial part of your financial life.

The use of credit, and specifically credit cards, has numerous benefits:

- **Convenience:** Credit cards are easy to use, especially for online transactions or travel. You can book flights or hotel rooms instantly.

- **Build Credit:** Using a credit card responsibly and making timely payments is the primary way to build a good credit score, which is essential for obtaining major loans such as mortgages.

- **Rewards:** Many credit cards offer rewards such as cashback, travel points, or discounts on purchases. This can be a great way to earn perks, like a free vacation, for purchases you would make anyway.

- **Fraud Protection:** Credit cards often provide better protection against fraudulent purchases than debit cards, which draw directly from your bank account.

Of course, there are also risks, which must be managed like any potential classroom distraction:

- **High-Interest Rates:** Credit cards typically have the highest interest rates of any financial product.

- **Debt Accumulation:** The ease of use and availability of credit can tempt users to overspend and accumulate debt beyond their means, leading to long-term financial stress.

- **Fees:** Credit cards often come with fees, such as annual fees, balance transfer fees, and late payment fees, which can add up quickly.

Credit and credit cards can be a powerful financial tool when used responsibly, but they also carry risks that must be carefully considered. If you can navigate students' use of cell phones in your school, which comes with its own benefits and challenges, you have the skills to navigate the world of credit as well.

REAL TEACHER TALK

Keep credit card debt to a minimum and don't just make minimum payments or you will never pay it off.

- Brenda (30 years as an educator)

Ways to Improve Your "GPA"

If a student asks you how they can improve their grade, what would you tell them? The advice is probably standard: be in class, pay attention, complete your work, ask for help, and study for the test. Am I right? Improving your credit score has similarly straightforward guidance, specifically aimed at the five components of your financial GPA:

- **Pay Your Bills On Time (35% of your Score):**

    - ○ **The Lesson:** Payment history is the most important factor in calculating your credit score. It is your attendance record for every financial obligation. Make sure you pay all of your bills on time, including credit card payments, loan payments, and utility bills. A single late payment can severely impact your score for years.

- **Reduce Your Credit Card Balances (30% of your Score):**

    - ○ **The Lesson:** This relates to your credit utilization ratio (i.e. how much of your available credit you are using). Keep your credit card balances low relative to your credit limit. Aim to use no more than 30% of your available credit, and ideally, keep it below

10%. Paying off your balance in full every month is the single best habit.

- **Be Cautious When Closing Old Credit Card Accounts (15% of your Score):**

  - **The Lesson:** Length of credit history is a factor in calculating your credit score. It is like your teaching tenure. Closing an old credit card account can shorten your credit history and lower your score. However, keeping an old card open just for the sake of your credit history, when that card is a temptation that causes you to spend more, is not worth it. Take the short-term hit to your score and eliminate the temptation.

- **Apply for Credit Sparingly (10% of your Score):**

  - **The Lesson:** Each time you apply for credit, it generates a "hard inquiry" which can temporarily lower your credit score. Avoid applying for multiple credit accounts at once. Avoid store credit cards like the plague; they often offer a small discount now but come with exorbitant interest rates. Have one or two good all-purpose rewards cards that you use responsibly.

- **Check Your Credit Report for Errors:**

  - **The Lesson:** As mentioned, errors on your credit report can hurt your credit score. Check your report regularly and dispute any errors with the credit bureaus immediately.

- **Consider a Secured Credit Card:**

  - **The Lesson:** If you have no credit history (you are a financial freshman) or a poor credit score, a secured credit card can help you establish or rebuild your credit. With this card, you make a deposit that serves as your credit limit, reducing the bank's risk. Use the card responsibly and make timely payments to improve your score.

Just like a student improving their grade in a class, improving your credit score takes time and discipline. In the world of credit scores, there is no one-time extra credit assignment that fixes everything. Success comes from the consistent, daily practice of good habits. Keep up these good practices, avoid credit card debt, and over time your score will improve, opening the door to a more secure and prosperous financial future.

EXTRA CREDIT: Did you know you can freeze your credit? If you will not apply for any new lines of credit in the immediate future, go to the three credit bureaus: Experian, Equifax, and TransUnion, and learn how to freeze your credit. This restricts access to your credit report, preventing new accounts from being opened in your name, which is a strong defense against identity theft. When the time comes to apply for a loan you can login and unfreeze your credit temporarily. Once the loan is secured, freeze it again to protect yourself.

Wallace

Housing: Your Financial Foundation

D o you feel like your classroom is your space? It did not matter whether I was in a room for a year or longer; it always felt like my home away from home, and I wanted it to reflect exactly what I wanted. Always clean and organized, filled with student work, content reminders, and inspirational quotes on the walls. I remember early on in my career a traveling teacher used my classroom during my prep period, and I "graciously" gave them one corner to decorate. Looking back, that was pretty selfish of me, as teaching from a cart is no one's idea of an ideal setup.

That need for a safe, organized, and personal space is exactly why your housing decision is the second most critical choice in your personal finance journey, just behind marriage.

Despite the popular and often frustrating advice that you can become a millionaire by cutting out your avocado toast or skipping your specialty coffee each day (to be honest, educators should not skip their morning coffee), your largest financial purchase of a home is far more likely to impact your financial life, for better or worse. Do not get me wrong, those small daily spending decisions are important and can add up over time. But all the savings from coffee and eating out will not matter if you make a poor housing decision that busts your budget. Housing is one of the Big Three expenses (Housing, Transportation, Food) that significantly impacts your financial future.

In this chapter, as we explore the financial implications of buying versus renting, a general rule is that housing costs should not exceed 30% of your net income (take-home pay). Traditionally, the 30% benchmark was all-inclusive, covering rent or mortgage, as well as insurance, utilities, and property taxes. Unfortunately, keeping housing expenses at or below this ratio has become increasingly difficult, especially for educators in high cost-of-living areas.

REAL TEACHER TALK

I live alone and live outside of my school district boundaries, where housing is cheaper.

- Marcia (13 years as an educator)

To Rent or Not to Rent, that is the Question

(Bonus points to those who recognized that line from *Hamlet*... an excellent example of literary retention!) Housing is one of the most significant expenses for individuals and families, including educators. Deciding whether to rent or buy is a crucial choice that requires careful consideration of various factors, often examined through a cost-benefit analysis.

Renting

Many people rent their housing at some point in adulthood. Renting provides flexibility and involves fewer financial responsibilities compared to owning a home.

Benefits (The Pros)	Drawbacks (The Cons)
Low Upfront Costs: You typically only need a security deposit and first month's rent. This is much smaller than a down payment, making renting accessible for educators with limited savings (the financial equivalent of having a smaller required reading list).	**No Equity/Asset Accumulation:** Rent payments do not build wealth or contribute to your net worth. The rent check is simply paying for the service of a roof over your head.

No Maintenance/Repairs: Landlords are responsible for property maintenance and repairs, relieving renters of unexpected expenses (your financial "sub plan" handles emergencies).	**Rent Increases:** Landlords can and often do increase rent prices annually, potentially making it challenging for educators to budget for housing costs over time.
High Mobility: Renting allows educators to easily relocate for job opportunities or changes in their personal lives without the hassle of selling a home.	**Limited Control:** Renters have limited control over the property and may face restrictions on customization or renovations. You cannot paint the walls or remodel the kitchen without permission.

Renting is not necessarily "throwing money away" because it provides a necessary service: shelter. However, that money does not contribute to building personal wealth. One exception is if you find a rental that is significantly cheaper than a comparable mortgage. In this situation, if you invest the difference between the rent and a potential mortgage payment, you could grow your equity not through housing, but through smart investment. This strategy requires the discipline of a seasoned veteran educator.

To Buy or Not to Buy, that is Also the Question

Buying a home is likely to be the largest financial decision you will make. You should approach each purchase with as much consideration as you give to supporting your students well.

High Upfront Costs

Purchasing a home requires a substantial initial investment in upfront costs, often the biggest hurdle for young educators.

- **Down Payment:** It used to be that a 20% down payment was required to purchase a home. However, with home prices rising faster than the typical educator's salary and the availability of a wider range of loan terms, a 20% down payment is no longer mandatory. As a teacher, you may qualify for lower mortgage rates or other favorable terms through programs offered by state or local teacher retirement systems designed to support educators. Before you start seriously looking, do your homework on your funding options.

- **Private Mortgage Insurance (PMI):** If you purchase a home with a traditional mortgage and put down less than 20% of the purchase price, you will likely need to pay for PMI. This insurance protects lenders in case you default on the loan. PMI adds an extra monthly cost until you build

20% equity in your home. Be sure to read the fine print before signing any loan agreements, as this is an additional fee to consider.

- **Closing Costs:** If you thought school fees were high, closing costs can be even more daunting. Closing costs include all the fees associated with securing a mortgage and completing the home purchase, such as appraisal fees, title fees, attorney fees, etc. These costs typically range from 2% to 5% of the loan amount.

Because of all these fees, a good rule of thumb is not to buy a home unless you plan to stay for at least five years. That timeframe allows you to take advantage of potential monthly savings and home appreciation, making the upfront costs worthwhile.

Home Buying Risks

Home values can fluctuate based on market conditions, affecting the potential for appreciation or loss. While housing prices generally rise over the long term, short-term declines do occur, such as during the Great Recession of the early 2000s. Prices can increase much more rapidly in economically booming areas than in stable or economically depressed regions. Just as you know your students better than a district administrator would, you understand your regional economy better than this book can explain. Do your homework.

Owning a home also reduces your flexibility as it ties you to a specific location. It is similar to signing your first teaching contract: you know you are committed there for a while, for better or worse. If you are unhappy with your job but your district is the only option nearby, it may not be the right time to put down roots by purchasing a home.

Home Buying Benefits

With those considerations out of the way, we can now focus on the substantial benefits of buying a home. For many, owning a home is part of the American dream, largely because of the financial advantages it offers:

- **Equity Accumulation:** When you rent, your monthly payment builds someone else's wealth. When you own a home, you experience equity accumulation. Homeownership allows individuals to build equity over time as they pay down their mortgage, with principal payments acting like a savings account as the property potentially appreciates in value. Your home is not only a shelter; it is also a growing asset that contributes to your net worth.

- **Financial Stability:** Owning a home provides stability and a sense of security. As long as you can make your payments, you do not have to worry about rent increases each year, which is especially beneficial for educators on a fixed-salary schedule. Increases in utilities and insurance will occur and need to be considered in your budgeting.

- **Tax Incentives:** The government offers incentives, similar to how teachers use incentives, to promote specific behaviors. In the United States, homeowners may benefit from tax deductions for mortgage interest and property taxes, which can reduce their overall tax liability.

REAL TEACHER TALK

I'm saving extra money to pay off my mortgage and go on vacations.

- Shauna (21 years as an educator)

Tax Deduction Opportunity

If your salary is $70,000 and you pay $5,000 in mortgage interest over the year, that deduction reduces your taxable income to $65,000 for the IRS, assuming you itemize on your federal taxes. With an example tax rate of 20%, you would save $1,000 in taxes ($5,000 deduction x 20% tax rate). The more you pay in mortgage interest and the higher your tax rate, the greater the tax savings. While these deductions alone are not a reason to buy a home instead of renting one, they are a helpful financial benefit for those who itemize deductions. Keep in mind that most educators do not itemize deductions on their taxes and instead take the standard deduction, which often results in greater savings.

Strategies for Housing Choices and Long-Term Planning

For educators weighing the rent versus buy decision, several financial strategies can help you make an informed choice.

- **The Cost-Benefit Analysis:** Compare the total costs of renting versus buying, including upfront expenses, monthly payments, and long-term financial implications such as potential appreciation versus investment returns. The split-second decision you make when deciding whether a student's behavior is worth correcting is a cost-benefit analysis. Apply the same logic when evaluating housing options.

- **Assess Affordability:** Calculate housing costs as a percentage of your income to ensure affordability and avoid becoming house poor, which occurs when you own a home but have little money left for other expenses. For educators this often means considering:
  - Do you have a significant other to contribute to costs?
  - Will you get a roommate?

o Are you willing to live in a less desirable location for a better price?

The Ultimate Goal: Mortgage Freedom by Retirement

If you are near retirement, I would argue that paying off your mortgage before you retire is a non-negotiable financial goal. Many people who do not do this, but they are not living the kind of financial life you probably want. When you retire, you will be living on a fixed income, which is likely smaller than your current earnings. Imagine how much further your monthly pension and retirement checks will go if you do not have to use them for mortgage payments.

If you are many years from retirement, consider your ability to pay off your mortgage early. Doing so not only saves a significant amount in interest over the life of the loan but also provides considerable mental comfort. Without a mortgage you gain financial freedom, and if you sell the house, all the proceeds belong to you.

EXTRA CREDIT: Look for an online mortgage calculator and play with the numbers. Compare the total interest paid on a 30-year mortgage versus a 15-year mortgage on a $250,000 loan at current interest rates. Notice how much more interest you will pay in the long run on the longer loan.

EXTRA CREDIT: If you currently have a mortgage, think of ways you can pay extra on your principal each month. Even adding just one extra principal payment a year (or one-twelfth of your principal payment each month) can shave years and tens of thousands of dollars off the life of your loan. This small, consistent effort mirrors the power of compounding—the eighth wonder of the world!

The decision to rent or buy a home is a major financial milestone for educators and requires careful consideration of personal circumstances, goals, and financial resources. You spend your days helping students, and you deserve to make a choice that benefits you both now and in the future. By evaluating the pros and cons and applying sound financial strategies, you can make informed housing decisions that align with your overall financial objectives.

Wallace

Pension & Retirement: Planning Beyond the Classroom

I once saw a well-intentioned meme on social media that said, "Teachers don't teach for the income; they teach for the outcome." While that is catchy, charming, and contains a fundamental truth, none of us work solely out of the goodness of our hearts. If we did, we would not need collective bargaining units, there would never be threats of strikes, and school boards would never have to worry about increasing our compensation.

Teaching and running schools is an essential profession. We educate the students who will one day run our businesses, tackle societal problems, and lead our government. Our future is in our hands, and most of us take that responsibility seriously. Society should treat us as the professionals we are, rather than using scare tactics to alarm parents by claiming that we are teaching ideologies that their favorite news channel has deemed harmful.

We teach for the outcomes, and we teach for the income. As educators, we understand that part of our total compensation package includes both income now and income in retirement. That guaranteed income in retirement is called a pension, and it is the single most stabilizing factor in an educator's financial life.

The Power of the Defined Benefit

Note: If you are a private school educator, you probably receive some sort of retirement match into a 403b or similar retirement plan but likely do not participate in a pension plan. The chapter on investing will be more relevant to you but I still encourage you to read and understand this chapter. I started out teaching in a private school before moving to public education. That could be your future too and the availability of a pension plan might be a key part of that decision making for you.

REAL TEACHER TALK

I wish someone had told me to attend a pension information workshop at the time of hire. I waited too long to clearly understand how my pension program worked.

- Sara (23 years as an educator)

Perhaps the strongest financial reason to become a public school educator is the opportunity to join the state teachers' retirement system. Fifty years ago, pensions existed across many career fields, but today they are mostly reserved for public service professionals. Just as we often work more than a 40-hour work week in exchange for the long breaks the school year provides, we accept salaries that are often lower than those of our college-educated peers in exchange for a secure, lifelong monthly check after retirement.

The data confirms this trade-off: the average public school teacher salary in 2025 was around $72,000. Compared to other similarly college-educated professionals, teachers earn about 73 cents on the dollar. That pension, which is part of your total compensation package, is designed to offset this teacher pay penalty. The fact that you qualify for a pension should excite you and make you grateful.

Most public school teachers participate in what is known as a "defined benefit" (DB) pension plan. Defined benefit plans promise a predetermined, specific benefit level of retirement income based on a formula. This is considered the gold standard of retirement because it represents a future income stream that cannot be outlived.

Compensation Type	Defined Benefit Plan (Pension)	Defined Contribution Plan (401k/403b)
Payer of Investment Risk	The State/Retirement System	The Employee/You
Benefit Guarantee	Guaranteed monthly payment for life based on formula.	Not guaranteed; depends on market performance and contribution.
Analogy	A guaranteed "A" in the class.	The grade depends solely on your test performance.

A Realistic Look at Pension Funding

Despite the security of a Defined Benefit plan, it is essential to be a realistic financial consumer. Concerns exist regarding the funding of state pension systems, the most significant being unfunded liabilities. The equation for calculating unfunded liabilities is: Unfunded Liability = Total Future Obligations - Current Assets.

Underfunding means there is currently insufficient money on the books, and not enough coming in to cover the full promises that have already been made to current and future educators. Across the

United States, the average public pension plan is funded at approximately 80% meaning that for every dollar promised to retirees, the system only holds only about 80 cents. This aggregate shortfall amounts to an estimated $1.5 trillion in pension debt.

However, there is no need to panic. Public pension systems have many legal protections, and any decreases in future benefits typically affect future contributors rather than those already vested in the system. While some states such as New York, Wisconsin, and South Dakota are nearly fully funded, others like Illinois and New Jersey are critically underfunded. Knowing the funded status of your state's pension provides a general indication of the health of your plan.

While a pension remains a powerful benefit, it is no longer the guaranteed safety net it once was, particularly since many teachers no longer spend their entire careers in a single system.

EXTRA CREDIT: If you teach in a public school and will receive a pension, look up your state teacher retirement system unfunded liability. Then see if you can find year-over-year data to see if that unfunded liability is decreasing or increasing. Finally, research what plan your state retirement system has in place to address the unfunded liability.

The Pension Calculation

Do you know how your pension benefit is calculated? If you do not, log onto your state teachers' retirement website and review their formula. A list of links to each state's teachers' retirement system is provided in the appendix.

The defined benefit formula works like a teaching weighted gradebook. Each component carries a specific weight, and increasing any one of them boosts your final outcome. Calculations vary by state but in general they follow these guidelines:

Annual Pension Benefit = Multiplier x Final Average Salary x Years of Service

- **The Multiplier:** This number is set by the pension plan, usually between 1.1% and 2.5%, and depends on the age at which the member retires. Similar to Social Security, the longer you wait to start receiving your monthly benefit, the larger that benefit will be. Delaying retirement effectively increases your multiplier in the formula.

- **Final Average Salary:** This is typically calculated using an average salary over a few years such as the highest 36 consecutive months of employment, or the "Highest 3 Years". This prevents employees from inflating their salary in a single year to permanently raise their monthly pension check. Educators can increase this factor by transferring to a higher-paying district, taking on additional stipend duties such as coaching or serving as department head, teaching summer school, or moving into administrative roles.

- **Years of Service:** This is based on time and sweat equity. A member cannot earn more than one year of service per school year. Each state plan sets a minimum number of years an educator must work in qualifying service to become eligible for benefits. On average, vesting requires around five years of qualifying service. The more years spent grading papers and creating classroom materials, the larger your monthly pension check will be.

Using a case study from the California State Teachers' Retirement System (CalSTRS), you can see how even small changes in the factors affect your monthly check at retirement.

Scenario	Retirement Age (Multiplier)	Highest Average Salary	Years Teaching	Monthly Benefit
Base Case	Age 60	$70,000	20	$2,333
Change 1 (Early Retirement)	Age 55	$70,000	20	$1,633

Change 2 **(Lower Salary)**	Age 60	$65,000	20	$2,166
Change 3 **(Less Service)**	Age 60	$70,000	15	$1,750

As you can see, a few hundred dollars difference in your monthly check adds up quickly. A $500 less a month benefit means a $30,000 difference in just five years of retirement. What could you do with an extra $30,000?

> **EXTRA CREDIT:** Pull up your pension system calculator and input the necessary information to calculate your retirement benefit. Try it once using current information, and try it again manipulating the numbers to the desired age you want to retire, what you think your ending salary will be, and how many years of service you think you will have.

The Retirement Tricycle

Now that you understand the basics of how your defined benefit plan works, it is critical to know that a pension alone is likely not enough for you to live comfortably in retirement.

Think of your retirement income as a three-wheeled Tricycle. The front wheel provides direction and stability, while the two back wheels provide propulsion and balance. If you are a private school educator, you are on a bicycle, with no pension to support you in retirement.

- **The Front Wheel:** Defined Benefit Pension Check. If you have enough years teaching, the defined benefit can be the building block of your retirement income. The average retired teacher in the U.S. receives an annual benefit of about $40,000 but that number can vary greatly. While substantial, this likely will not cover a comfortable retirement lifestyle, which is why you need the back wheels.

- **Back Wheel 1:** Social Security (SSI) Check.

- **Back Wheel 2:** Personal Retirement Account Withdrawals (403b, 457b, IRA, etc.)

We will now look more closely at the two back wheels.

Back Wheel 1: Social Security and the 35-Year Rule

Social Security was established in 1935 by President Franklin D. Roosevelt as "old age insurance." For more information on the history of Social Security (and some great primary documents for a history report), go to the Social Security Administration's history page at www.ssa.gov/history. As a former history teacher, I rarely pass up the chance to share a history lesson!

In 1935, the average life expectancy was 61, and the retirement age was 65. Today, the full retirement age is 67, but life expectancy is around 78, and there are fewer than three active workers for every one retiree. You do not have to be a math major to see that the numbers for the long-term viability of Social Security are not in our favor. If nothing changes, the Social Security trust fund reserves are expected to run out sometime around 2034, after which time it will only be able to pay approximately 80% of the benefits retirees are calculated to receive.

It is important to include Social Security as part of your financial plan. SSA benefits are calculated based on your 35 highest earning years. If you do not have 35 years of earnings, any missing years are calculated as zeros. We have all calculated enough gradebooks to know what a few zeros here and there can do to the final grade. My advice is to replace as many of those zeros as possible with years of salary.

No More Weeping over the WEP

Here is the kicker with Social Security for some of you: you need to check whether you pay into Social Security as a teacher or if your earnings are non-creditable. Approximately 40% of public school educators in the United States do not pay into the Social Security system. If you taught in California, as I did, your earnings were non-creditable. On the other hand, as a public school educator in Wisconsin and Montana, I paid into both the state retirement system and Social Security.

You should already know whether public school educators in your state pay into Social Security because you should be reading and understanding your pay stub each month.

For the educators in those 40% of non-contributing states, the Windfall Elimination Provision (WEP) used to significantly reduce their benefits. Think of the WEP as a penalty for being a "part-time" contributor to the Social Security system while receiving a generous full-time pension.

However, after many years of advocacy, in 2025, the Social Security Fairness Act was signed into law by President Biden, repealing the WEP. For the 40% of educators who earned Social Security credit from previous private-sector jobs or summer work, this repeal means you no longer have to worry about the penalty reducing your Social Security benefit by hundreds of dollars a month. It is a major win for educators, replacing a penalty with fairness.

EXTRA CREDIT: If you have not already done so, go to www.ssa.gov/myaccount and create an account. This will be your official online presence with Social Security, so make sure you choose a secure password. Review your earnings record and your projected benefit amount based on your age at retirement.

Back Wheel 2: Retirement Account Withdrawal Rate

In the chapter on investing, you will learn more about different types of investment accounts such as your 403b, 457b, or IRA, and where you should be putting extra money that can grow over time to support your retirement.

For planning purposes, financial experts generally rely on the 4% Rule as a guideline for a sustainable withdrawal rate. Developed from the famous Trinity Study, the 4% Rule is a guideline that suggests withdrawing 4% of your retirement portfolio's value each year to help ensure that your money lasts for at least 30 years, even during market volatility. Think of this rule as your pacing guide for retirement spending.

It is important to know the amount you need or want to live off from your retirement accounts so that you can determine how much you need to save. Let us do some math to find your Magic Number:

According to the 4% Rule your savings goal = annual withdrawal need x 25 (The number 25 is the multiplicative inverse of 0.04).

Example:

1. **Determine your shortfall:** Let us say after you calculate your pension monthly check and your Social Security monthly check, you determine you will need an additional $2,000 a month to live the lifestyle you want.

2. **Calculate Annual Need:** $2,000 x 12 months = $24,000 per year

3. **Calculate Savings Goal (Magic Number):** $24,000 x 25 = $600,000

This means you need to have $600,000 invested in your retirement accounts by the time you retire to safely generate the extra $2,000 per month you want, on top of your guaranteed income streams. It is important to note that the 4% rule is not a guarantee, but rather a guideline based on historical market data.

EXTRA CREDIT: What is your Magic Amount? If you completed the extra credit exercises in this chapter and have an idea of how much your pension and Social Security will be, take an educated guess at how much you will need each month versus how much you will realistically want each month. If your guaranteed income sources do not cover your wants, calculate how much more you will want each month. Then, do the math as outlined above (multiply the annual shortfall by 25) to see how much you will need to have invested to fund the life you desire.

Insurance: Managing Risk

As the saying goes, insurance feels like a waste of money until you need it. Your students might feel similarly about the information you present them in class. They do not think they need it until it appears on a test. But just as studying helps students prepare for unexpected exam questions, insurance helps you prepare for life's unpredictable moments. In this chapter we will discuss the various types of insurance available to the public, including one insurance product specifically geared toward educators.

Insurance is a bit like sub plans. You do not give them much thought until you need them and then you hope they are good enough that your time away is not a complete disaster. It is the same with insurance. Once you choose a policy, most people rarely think about it again until the policy is up for renewal or the monthly bill arrives.

The most common types of insurance are home or renters insurance, auto insurance, life insurance, and health insurance.

In this book we will not cover health insurance as it is typically provided by your employer and coverage depends on their offerings and how much they pay towards it. If you are a young educator you might still be on your parents' health insurance, but that will not always be the case. If you are an experienced educator, you likely already understand the importance and value of good health insurance. The bottom line is to make sure you have health insurance and make sure you understand your benefits.

Home or Renters Insurance

Home or renters' insurance covers not only the structure of your dwelling and its contents but also covers your liability if someone is injured while visiting. Americans are often quick to sue and it is a sad reality that we all need protection in case something happens in our homes. In the event of an emergency or a crisis, the last thing you want to worry about is how to pay to replace your house or belongings. Adequate insurance coverage gives you one less thing to worry about while you rebuild.

When I was an administrator for a large school system in California, I saw many staff members lose their homes to natural disasters such as wildfires or floods. We always rallied around them but those with adequate home insurance could focus on coping with the event rather than worrying about the cost of rebuilding.

How much coverage is enough? That depends on the value of your home and its contents. The more valuable your home and belongings, the more insurance you will need. Most insurance brokers are thorough in analyzing your home and needs. Think of brokers as guidance counselors, they want to understand enough about you to put you in the right policy.

Auto Insurance

Auto insurance provides financial protection to vehicle owners in case of accidents or other unforeseen events involving their cars. If you ever drive your car for school purposes, your school or district likely has minimum insurance requirements. Auto insurance is essential, especially if you drive frequently as it is one of the most likely types of insurance you may need to use. It typically covers damages caused to other people's property or injuries to others in an accident caused by the insured driver.

There are several types of coverage options available under an auto insurance policy. Depending on your state, different coverage types and minimum coverage levels may be required. Generally, liability coverage is required by law although the minimum coverage levels vary. Some common coverage types include:

- liability coverage

- collision coverage

- comprehensive coverage

- personal injury protection

- uninsured/underinsured motorist coverage

- roadside assistance

- glass replacement

If your budget is tight and you drive an older car, it may make financial sense to forgo collision and comprehensive coverage. Sometimes the premiums for these coverages are not worth the benefit they provide because your vehicle may not be worth much to repair or replace in the event of a claim. Collision coverage handles damage from impacts with other vehicles or objects while comprehensive coverage protects against unexpected damage such as theft, falling tree branches, or hitting an animal. A good rule of thumb is that if the premium cost for either coverage exceeds 10% of your vehicle's value, it may not be worth it. These coverages only pay the current market value of your vehicle at the time of the incident. For example, if your $5,000 car costs more than $500 a year to insure for collision or comprehensive coverage, or the deductible exceeds $500, it may be financially wise to drop that coverage, provided you have a strong emergency fund to pay for repairs or replacement out of pocket.

The cost of your auto insurance premium depends on factors such as your age, driving record, the type of vehicle you own, and the coverage options you choose. The deductible is the amount you pay out of pocket before your insurance coverage kicks in. Higher deductibles generally result in lower premiums. If you are early in your career, still paying off college loans, surviving on leftovers from the teacher's lounge, and working a second job just to make ends meet, you may need a lower deductible because you likely do not have a large emergency fund to cover a car accident.

One of the benefits of an emergency fund is that you have access to cash in case of an emergency, and a vehicle accident qualifies. Once you have a healthy emergency fund and your budget is under control, consider raising your deductible. Although you will pay more if you file a claim, your premiums will be lower overall.

Many auto insurance companies offer discounts to their customers, such as safe driver discounts, multi-car discounts, and bundling discounts. If you have more than one driver in your household, it is best to have everyone on the same policy. It may also help you to have your home or renters insurance through the same company as your auto insurance. This can provide an additional discount and simplify the payment and claims process.

Some companies offer professional discounts to licensed educators. While I do not think educators are inherently safer drivers than the general population, these discounts have a long history. Check your insurance statement or contact your insurance company to see if you are receiving the educator discount. If not, request it and be prepared to provide a copy of your educator license.

EXTRA CREDIT: If it has been two or more years since you last shopped around for your home and auto insurance policies, set aside time, perhaps on a school break, to check prices. Did you know you can switch insurance companies at any time? It does not just have to be at renewal time. You will get a prorated refund for the amount remaining on your premium if you switch mid-term. Insurance prices vary widely and change often. Do not let your loyalty to one company keep you locked into paying more. I check every few years and often end up switching companies and save hundreds of dollars a year in doing so. If you have had any major life changes such as a new car or moving, that is also a good time to look for new coverage. Find an insurance broker that will compare prices at many different insurance companies all at once. Never go to an insurance agent for a single company as they will only quote you the price for coverage at their company which may or may not be the best deal. A quick internet search for "auto insurance broker" or "home insurance broker" will give you a list of local and online brokers you can reach out to.

Life Insurance

Working with students keeps us young. Though I am quickly moving through middle age, I am more familiar with the social media habits and constantly changing slang of adolescents than most people my age. You probably know the latest books and shows and clothing preferences of youth, even if you are still wearing the same free t-shirt you received during your first year of teaching. Yet despite how young at heart you are, part of being financially savvy is planning for your future, including the worst case scenario of your untimely death.

Many school systems provide life insurance for their employees. You might think this is enough and maybe it is. Consider your situation. The purpose of life insurance is to provide income to loved ones after your death. If you are single and have no dependents, you probably do not need life insurance. If you have a family or others who rely on you, life insurance is an important protection. The life insurance provided to you by your school is a nice benefit, but it only covers you if you die while employed by the school system.

So where does that leave you?

Most financial experts recommend term life insurance. Term life insurance provides coverage for a specified period of time, typically between 10 and 30 years. You generally pay annually, and the policy covers you regardless of where you work. It is more affordable than permanent life insurance and is a good option for people who need coverage for a specific period of time, such as until their children are grown or until their mortgage is paid off. After a certain point in life you may no longer need to leave as much money to your heirs, so your life insurance coverage can be reduced or eliminated.

As an educator I assume you are not rolling in money and do not need complicated life insurance arrangements. If someone tries to sell you whole life or universal life or variable life insurance, these are all known as permanent life insurance options and they are not for you. They are complicated and expensive. Run away as if the recess bell just rang.

To determine how much life insurance you need, consider your current financial situation, debts, income, and future financial obligations. A good rule of thumb is to have coverage that is equal to about 10 times your annual income. However, this may vary based on your specific circumstances.

Term life insurance rates increase the older you are when you secure the coverage. Early in my 20s, when I was single and just starting out as a private school teacher, I could not afford nor did I need life insurance because no one depended on me for their survival (besides the 7th graders desperately trying to learn pre-algebra). I understand if you are early in your educational career and find the thought of life insurance daunting, both because it forces you to consider your untimely death and because it adds another expense to your meager starting salary.

If that is the case, file this information away. Someday you may need term life insurance and in the unfortunate event it is used, your heirs will thank you for taking care of them even after you are gone.

Professional Liability Insurance

I have been in education long enough to see how society's perception of teachers changes. Some view us as heroes who are asked to put ourselves between our students and harm from the next school shooter. Others see us as groomers and indoctrinators who seek to brainwash their children. When people make these accusations, I wryly respond that I cannot even get my students to turn in homework, so I think they are overstating my ability to indoctrinate children. Our standing in society can change quickly and it is important to protect yourself.

Teaching is a profession where professional liability insurance makes sense. This type of insurance is an insurance policy that provides coverage to professionals against lawsuits and claims that arise from their professional services.

When I was a senior level school administrator, I spent an inordinate amount of time consulting with legal counsel to prevent or address potential lawsuits. Most threats were related to special education but certainly not all. Once, a parent took our school to small claims court because we would not allow the family to keep the school computer and other curriculum. I quickly learned that anyone can sue for any reason, regardless of merit.

Educators, like other professionals, may want to consider obtaining professional liability insurance to protect themselves against claims or lawsuits related to their work. This insurance can help cover the costs of legal fees, settlements, or judgments related to any alleged negligence, errors, or omissions in teaching.

While professional liability insurance is not mandatory, it may be worth considering, especially if you work in a litigious environment or with vulnerable populations. If you are a part of a teachers' union, you may already have coverage. Check with your union to confirm whether it is included with your dues.

The cost of individual teacher's professional liability coverage is typically affordable, often ranging from $100 to $300 per year. Considering the rising legal scrutiny educators face, you must determine if the cost is worth the peace of mind that comes with knowing your legal fees are covered in case of an alleged error, omission, or negligence claim.

I am not saying professional liability coverage is a must, but in a personal finance book for educators, I would be remiss not to mention it as an option to consider to protect yourself financially.

EXTRA CREDIT: If you are part of a union, check to see if your membership includes liability coverage. If you are not part of a union, some non-union teaching organizations provide educators with liability coverage as part of their membership. Do an internet search to find one you might be interested in joining and see how much it costs.

Investing: Growing Long-Term Wealth

T his chapter is a long one. It is time to put all those great reading strategies you have used with students over the years to work. Chunk the reading. Activate your prior knowledge. Preview the text. Annotate!

PEMDAS for Investing

Please Excuse My Dear Aunt Sally that easy-to-remember saying helps students understand the order of operations (Parenthesis Exponents Multiplication/Division Addition/Subtraction). Students cannot progress past a certain level in math without mastering this concept. Investing has an order of operations too. You have many ways to invest your money, but what is the best way for you to invest your limited funds?

Think of your investment journey like the scope and sequence you carefully plan for your students. You would not throw a fifth-grader straight into college-level physics, right? You need to master the foundational units first. Investing works the same way. You need a clear, sequenced plan to ensure your hard-earned dollars work as efficiently as possible. This sequence helps you capture the most significant financial benefits first, maximizing your return on effort, much like scaffolding a complex lesson to ensure student success.

Your Investment Steps

If you are a public school educator, you probably have money automatically deducted as part of your pension. Most workers, including private school educators, are not so lucky. For those of us in public education, the pension is one of the benefits we receive for choosing a life of public service in classrooms with too many student needs and too few resources. In most states employees contribute a portion of their income to the pension, and in most cases this is automatic. So let us focus on the types of investing you control. Your pension is a dependable, non-negotiable benefit that provides a guaranteed level of income.

Regardless of whether you have a pension or not, your goal should be to invest 20% of your gross income. Remember your gross income is the amount you earn from the salary scale before taxes or other deductions.

Step 1: Employer Match (Free Money)

First, if you receive a 403b (or 401k or 457) investment match from your employer, invest your money there, up to the match. These accounts are set up through your employer and someone in your Human Resources or Benefits department can help you. Receiving a match for your 403b contributions is unlikely for public school educators because the school already puts money into your retirement through the pension system. If you work at a private K-12 school or private university you are more likely to have a match option. When your employer matches the money you put into your 403b account, that is essentially free money for you.

To not contribute enough to get the employer match is like leaving the extra credit question blank on a test. Worse, it is like being offered a bonus point for simply writing your name on the paper and refusing to do so. For many private sector workers, the match is an automatic return on your investment. You put in $1, and your employer instantly gives you matching money. That is a positive investment gain before the market even moves! Studies show that anywhere from one-quarter to one-third all workers do not contribute enough to capture their full employer match. Do not be one of them.

For example, if your school matches 50% of your contributions, up to three percent, you should contribute 6% of your income to maximize the 3% match from your employer. If you earn $50,000 a year, that 3% match is an additional $1,500 your employer gives you for extra credit, to be used in retirement.

Step 2: Roth IRA (The Teacher's Pet)

After hitting your 403b (or 401k or 457) account match (Step 1), your next move should be to contribute the maximum into your Roth Individual Retirement Account (IRA). While everyone's financial situation is unique, I generally recommend opening a Roth IRA rather than a traditional IRA. In a Roth account the money goes in post-tax, but when you withdraw it after age 59.5, both contributions and earnings are tax free.

In a traditional IRA, as in a 403b, the money goes in pre-tax. You do not pay taxes on the money when it is deposited, but you pay taxes on the contributions and earnings when you withdraw in retirement. I fund my Roth IRA every year. True to their name, IRAs are individual retirement accounts, so you will need to open one through a low cost brokerage. More on this later in this chapter.

Step 3: Health Savings Account (HSA)

If you still have money in your budget to invest after the first two steps, and you have access to a Health Savings Account (HSA) through work, that should be your next option for investment. The trick with an HSA is that your health plan must be a High-Deductible Plan (HDHP) in order to qualify.

Having a HDP typically means you pay the full cost of your healthcare out of pocket until you reach the deductible. To help offset this cost the government created HSAs, allowing employees to contribute pre-tax money that can then be taken out to pay for qualified medical expenses. HSA's can also be saved and invested and they are considered triple tax free. More on this later in this chapter.

Step 4: Max Out 403b/401k/457 (Exceeds Expectations)

The fourth investing step is to return to your 403b (or 401k or 457) and continue contributing there up to the maximum allowed by law. Few people hit the maximum contribution limit, which is over $20,000. Once you reach 50 years of age, catch-up contributions bring the total you can contribute to over $30,000 for the year. You see how out of reach this is for most educators, even for those who are financially savvy. If you are able to contribute that much of your salary to a retirement account, you should be writing this book. I have had years where I paid into a pension system and social security and maxed out my Roth IRA and contributed to a 403b, but I have never been able to reach the maximum while juggling all the other expenses of life.

According to a recent study by two of the largest brokerage firms in the United States, less than 15% of workers across all fields are able to do this. In the education field, the percentage is even lower. Given educators' salaries in the United States, the likelihood of being able to max out an IRA, HSA, and a 403b/401k/457 is extremely low.

REAL TEACHER TALK

I have CD's, a 403b, IRA, investment property, and a High Yield Savings Account...I hope to retire, live on a beach, and just write!

- Jon (28 years as an educator)

Investing Gravy: 529 and Taxable Brokerage

If you have completed the first four steps you are already ahead of the class. Anything beyond that point is investing gravy. At this stage consider opening a 529 college investment account if you have children, or a taxable brokerage account. In a 529 account the money grows tax-free and can be used tax-free on qualified educational expenses for the person named on the account or for a family member of that named person.

You might be thinking, "I am an educator who loves children and wants to put my kids first". Yes, as an educator and parent your children are a top priority. But remember, they can take out loans for college. There are no loans for retirement. Pay yourself first, then prepay their future expenses if there is anything left over.

Taxable brokerage accounts are similar to IRAs in that you have to open one at an investment firm of your choice. There are no investment or income limits, but there are also no tax benefits, so any gains that happen in the funds you buy mean owe taxes on a portion of that income each year. Brokerage accounts also make your tax filing process more complex. However, if you want to retire early, before you can access your Roth IRA or 403b or even pension, you can withdraw money from a taxable brokerage account at any time. Many early retirees use taxable brokerage accounts as a bridge, providing income until their pension begins or they can withdraw from tax-favored retirement accounts.

Pre-tax vs. Post-tax Investing

When I first started teaching, school retirement plans were only available on a pre-tax basis. The post-tax option was through a Roth IRA which individuals had to set up on their own. Today, most school systems offering a retirement plan give educators the choice of pre-tax or post-tax investing. This applies to schools without a pension system that contribute to the retirement plan, as well as schools with optional retirement plans but do not contribute to them because the school already contributes to your pension.

Pre-tax and post-tax investing refer to investment accounts that allow you to either defer taxes or pay taxes upfront. Each type of account has its own benefits.

Benefits of Pre-Tax Investing:

- **Lower taxes in the present:** Contributions to pre-tax accounts like a traditional 403b are made with pre-tax dollars, which can lower your taxable income in the present. This can help you save money on taxes now. For example, you may invest $250 into your pre-tax account but your actual take home pay may only be lowered by $50, because that money was taken out of your paycheck before taxes were applied. Pre-tax accounts are generally better for those with high incomes and/or those living in high tax states.

- **Tax-deferred growth:** Earnings on pre-tax investments grow tax-deferred until you withdraw them in retirement. This means you will not have to pay taxes on your investment gains until you withdraw the money.

Benefits of Post-Tax Investing:

- **Tax-free withdrawals:** Contributions to post-tax accounts, usually called the "Roth" version of the same pre-tax account, such as a Roth 403b or Roth IRA are made with after-tax dollars, which means you have already paid taxes on the money. This means you can withdraw your contributions and earnings tax-free in retirement.

- **Tax diversification:** By investing in post-tax accounts, you can create tax diversification in your retirement portfolio. This means you will have different types of accounts with different tax treatments, which can help you manage your taxes in retirement. So for example, your pension income will be taxed but the money you pull out of your Roth would not be.

You are going to pay taxes one way or another. As educators, we should not view taxes as bad. They fund our salaries and cover most of what goes into educating our students. Ultimately, the decision to invest in pre-tax or post-tax accounts depends on your individual financial situation.

A simple rule of thumb for deciding between pre-tax and post-tax retirement accounts is to consider whether you expect your taxes to be higher or lower in retirement than they are now. If you expect taxes to be higher in retirement, you should pay the taxes now and invest in post-tax options. If you expect taxes to be lower in retirement, investing in pre-tax options may serve you well. Keep in mind that for pre-tax accounts you eventually pay taxes on both your investment contributions and any earnings. For post-tax accounts you pay taxes on the money you invest but not on any earnings when you withdraw, as long as you have reached retirement age.

Now I know what you are thinking. Our government has growing and unsustainable levels of debt. Our nation continues to spend beyond its means, and eventually we are likely to see tax increases to cover expenses already incurred. That is true. I am not a betting person but if I were, I would bet we will see tax increases in our lifetime.

However, your tax rate is not just about the federal income tax rate. We have a progressive income tax system in this country, as do most states, where the more a person or family earns, the higher their tax rate. Federal and most state income tax rates are structured in brackets based on income.

So, the answer to whether your taxes in retirement will be higher or lower than you pay now is not necessarily simple. For example, if you are an administrator earning a solid salary or are married to someone with a high income, a tax break now may be worth it because those high salaries will likely be gone once you stop working. In theory most people earn less in retirement than they do as full time workers. A lower income in retirement may place you in a lower tax bracket.

Other factors can also affect your taxes in retirement. If you [;an to move to another state after retirement, perhaps to be near your children, pay lower taxes, or enjoy more sun, that could change your tax burden. A significant increase in the federal tax rate could offset these considerations. Ultimately, we cannot know for certain, so you must make your best, educated guess.

If you want to know what I do, as a middle-class earner, I always choose the post-tax option when available. I prefer to pay the income taxes now, while I have control over my earnings, rather than later when I may not be able to simply work more or find a higher paying job to cover the taxes.

Retirement Plan Options

403b

Most teachers have access to a 403b. This plan is similar to a 401k but is designed for workers in the non-profit sector. If you work for a for-profit educational entity you may be offered a 401k instead. For all intents and purposes the two plans are very similar and what you read in this section can also provide useful knowledge for your 401k options. Both can be offered as pre-tax or post-tax options. Both have the same contribution limit and the same minimum age for withdrawing money without a 10% tax penalty, which is 59.5 years old.

However, there are some minor differences between the two options. 403bs are less likely to offer employee matching funds due to additional regulations. If you do not have a pension that your school contributes to on your behalf, getting a match on your retirement contributions is an important component of your compensation package and overall retirement planning. If you are applying for a non-pensioned education job, do not overlook the organization's retirement contribution amount.

403bs may also offer fewer investment choices and higher fees than a 401k plan. The good news is that in many cases the non-profit organization (i.e. your school district) cannot limit the employees options to just one 403b plan. Choice is generally a good thing, but it is only helpful if the options are solid. Because some 403b plans do not have to meet a fiduciary standard, they can include high fees or low-quality products. A recent report by the Government Accountability Office found that 403b plan fees vary widely with some being 100% to 300% higher than the lowest-cost plans available in the marketplace. Over a career this can cost educators tens of thousands of dollars.

Most of the people who come to your teachers' lounge offering free pizza to talk about their products are salespeople whose goal is to make money off of you.

This is not to say you should not invest. You should. For most of us our pensions alone will not be enough to live comfortably off in retirement. So what can you do? Look for the plan with the lowest fees. Request a fee schedule and compare the 403b plan options available to you.

> **EXTRA CREDIT:** check out www.403bwise.org. It has much more information about 403b concerns and steps you can take to protect your financial future. Much like this book, the website is run by former educators who care about helping teachers be financially savvy.

457

As an educator, you may also have access to a 457 Plan. A 457 plan is a type of retirement account available to certain employees of state and local governments, as well as some non-profit organizations. This type of plan is also sometimes called a deferred compensation plan.

Like a 403b, 457 plans can be either pre-tax or post-tax. They generally offer a broader range of investments and they have a unique feature that allows employees to contribute more than the annual limits of other retirement plans, as long as they are within three years of the plan's normal retirement age. Unfortunately unless you earn a salary far above the national teacher average, it is unlikely you will reach the maximum contribution amount for any employer sponsored plan. Therefore, the ability to contribute more in the final three years before retirement may not be a significant incentive for the average educator.

What may be an incentive to you is that with a 457 plan you can withdraw funds earlier without the 10% early withdrawal tax penalty that applies to IRA, 403b, and 401k accounts. Remember that for 403b and IRA plans withdrawals before age 59.5 incur a penalty. With a 457 plan, you can withdraw funds penalty free, before age 59.5, as long as you have left the employer through which the plan was sponsored. Just like an emergency drill, you have to exit first.

Working with students day in and day out can be exhausting, so If you plan to retire before 59.5 and will need access to your investment accounts, you should seriously consider contributing to a 457 plan as a supplementary retirement option alongside your pension. Personally I prefer the 457 plan over the 403b when both options are offered. I do not plan to retire before 59.5 but life does not always go as expected, and I value the flexibility it provides.

If you do not plan to access the funds until after 59.5, then choose between a 403b or 457 based on which plan offers the best investment options and lowest fees. If your employer provides a retirement contribution match for one plan, choose that one as contribution matches are essentially free money and usually outweigh any higher fees the plan may charge.

Roth IRA

Have your students ever asked what is the best thing they can do to pass your class? In the world of personal finance, the Roth IRA is it. Beyond your pension or any organizational match on a school sponsored retirement account, the Roth IRA is one of the best investment options available.

An IRA is an Individual Retirement Account that belongs to you, not the school. You can set one up and keep it no matter where you work or move. The "Roth" IRA is a post-tax account which means you contribute money that has already been taxed. This also means that withdrawals in retirement are tax-free. Considering the investment growth potential, this can result in significant long-term tax savings.

Roth IRAs share the same minimum age for withdrawals without a tax penalty as 403b and 401k accounts, which is 59.5. However, Roth IRAs offer exceptions that provide greater flexibility. For instance, you can withdraw money tax- and penalty-free after the account has been open for five years, if funds are used for a first-time home purchase, college expenses, or birth or adoption related costs.

There is even more flexibility. Account owners can withdraw the contributions made to a Roth IRA (but not the earnings) tax- and penalty-free at any time after holding the account for five years.

These exceptions make it easier to access your retirement money before age 59.5, without penalties or taxes, as long as the rules are followed.

However, I strongly caution against early withdrawals. Retirement accounts are meant for retirement. If your students cash in all their good behavior tickets too soon, they may get a small amount of immediate gratification, but they miss out on bigger rewards at the end of the term. Similarly, withdrawing money early reduces the amount you will have when your paychecks stop.

While the flexibility of the Roth IRA is a valuable safety net in case of emergencies, you should only access the funds in genuine financial need. This is yet another reason why having an emergency fund of cash available is important. Your future self will thank you for letting the money grow as long as possible.

Additionally, Roth IRAs do not have Required Minimum Distributions (RMDs). Unlike traditional IRA, 403b, and 401k accounts, Roth IRAs do not force you to withdraw funds at a certain age. This allows your investments to continue growing tax-free for as long as you want. Roth IRAs are also an effective estate planning tool, as your beneficiaries can inherit the account tax-free, after your death. Imagine if our top students could carry over their extra credit points into another class, or pass it along to a friend.

That would be a pretty sweet deal for them. The Roth IRA is a sweet deal for you.

Because you open a Roth IRA yourself, regardless of your workplace, you get to choose the investment company. That means you can select one with low fees and the types of investments that fit your goals. Roth IRAs offer a wide range of investment options, including stocks, bonds, mutual funds, and exchange-traded funds (ETFs). This variety helps you diversify your portfolio and manage risk.

Have I convinced you yet? The best time to open a Roth IRA was last semester, but the next best time to do it is now. If you are unsure where to invest, start with three of the largest investment companies known for low fees. Remember, you can open a Roth IRA through many financial institutions but because this is such a valuable investment and funding it to the maximum each year should be a financial priority, choose a company that provides the investments you need at a low cost. Three of the biggest players in the consumer investment field are Vanguard, Fidelity, and Charles Schwab.

Roth IRAs are so advantageous that the government limits annual contributions. You can also only contribute if your income, or your household income if married and filing jointly, is below a certain threshold. These accounts are designed for lower- and middle-class households, which makes educators a perfect demographic to take advantage of Roth IRA benefits. The annual contribution limit changes each year but is currently below $10,000. Assuming you meet the income requirements, this can be an achievable goal for many educators.

HSA

A Health Savings Account (HSA) is a tax-advantaged savings account that you can use to pay for qualified medical expenses. You might be wondering why I included a section about health spending in the investment chapter. Well, why is the lunch period so short? Or why are students especially wild during a full moon? Some things remain a mystery, but this is not. If you have access to an HSA, it can be used as a powerful investment vehicle for you.

Your choice of health insurance is very personal and should be made with careful thought. Traditionally benefits for educators have been strong, often compensating for lower salaries. Sadly benefits have eroded over the years. Still, many school systems provide employees with a choice in the type of medical coverage for themselves and their family.

HSAs are typically paired with high-deductible health plans (HDHP), which have lower monthly premiums than traditional health insurance plans. By opting for an HDHP with an HSA, you may save money on your monthly insurance premiums. However, as the name implies, an HDHP has a high deductible, which means you must pay a significant amount out-of-pocket before your insurance coverage begins. Some refer to HDHPs as disaster plans because they only start paying claims once a high threshold of expenses has already been incurred and paid out of pocket by the employee.

If you are young or generally healthy, choosing a HDHP and putting the premium savings into your HSA may be a smart move. Some schools even contribute to your HSA on your behalf.

If you or your family members require regular medical care, a traditional plan, though it has higher monthly premiums (unless your school still covers the full cost) may save you money over the course of the year. It is okay to switch plans from year to year. I know young teachers who choose an HDHP because they are generally healthy, and want to pocket the premium savings. But then when they become pregnant they switch to a traditional health plan the following year to reduce out-of-pocket costs when their child is born.

Now that we have covered some of the background on HSAs, let us explore why you might want to consider opening one as part of your investment strategy.

- **Tax Benefits:** HSA contributions are pre-tax and tax-deductible, which lowers your taxable income by

Wallace

contributing to an HSA. Additionally, withdrawals from an HSA for qualified medical expenses are tax-free, further reducing your tax burden. You can also invest your HSA funds in the stock market. Both contributions and gains used for qualified medical expenses are tax-free. This makes HSAs triple tax-free.

- **Long-Term Savings:** Unlike flexible spending accounts (FSAs), HSAs have no "use it or lose it" rule. Any funds you contribute to an HSA can roll over from year to year, and can be invested to grow tax-free over time. This makes an HSA a useful tool for long-term healthcare planning.

- **Greater Control Over Healthcare Costs:** Using an HSA to pay for medical expenses gives you greater control over your healthcare spending. You can shop around for the best prices on non-urgent medical procedures, potentially saving money.

- **Money Passes to Heirs:** If you die, your HSA account rolls over to a spouse or heir. As long as the funds are used for medical expenses, they remain tax-free for them. This differs from an FSA which follows the use-it-or-lose-it rule.

Overall, an HSA can be a smart choice for anyone who wants to save on healthcare costs, reduce their tax burden, and gain more control over their medical spending. My family used a HDHP for five years. We contributed to our HSA each month but rarely used it for medical expenses. We chose to pay for medical costs out of pocket, and treat our HSA as an investment vehicle, letting the funds grow to cover expenses in retirement. There will be plenty of medical costs by then. However, if something unexpected occurs and we need extra money for medical bills, we can withdraw from our HSA at any time.

You might not be in a position to contribute to retirement accounts and an HSA while paying for current medical expenses. That is okay. Only about 20% of people with an HSA use it as an investment vehicle to save and grow funds for future expenses. The vast majority use it as a clearing account to put the money in for the tax deduction, then withdraw the money to cover current medical expenses. If you can afford an HDHP, fund your HSA, and invest over time, an HSA is an excellent savings vehicle for future healthcare needs.

REAL TEACHER TALK

I contribute to other retirement accounts as I hope to be able to retire after 30 years of teaching and be able to pay for healthcare while living the same lifestyle I'm living now with some additional travels before it's simply too late in life.

- Becky (27 years as an educator)

Risk Tolerance

I have always admired those teachers who could let their class teeter on the edge of losing control, yet had the skill to bring the class back in order to continue the lesson when necessary. Those teachers had a higher risk tolerance than I do. I am much more comfortable with ordered chaos in the classroom, which I hope makes you smile at least a little, because we all know that chaos is only one student action, comment, or [moment of disengagement away.

Like your classroom management, each of us has a risk tolerance level when it comes to investing. How much risk are you comfortable taking? Or to put it another way, how much of your money would you be okay losing in a down market before you panicked and pulled it out? Your risk tolerance is a personal decision that depends on your investment objectives, financial situation, time horizon, and emotional disposition toward risk. In general the greater the risk, the greater the potential reward.

To determine your risk tolerance, consider factors such as your age, income, investment goals, time horizon until you plan to start using the money, and current and future financial obligations.

At some point you may want to consult a financial advisor who can help assess your risk tolerance and develop a suitable investment strategy. Keep in mind that a financial advisor may either charge a fee or will sell products that generate income for them,so choose wisely. Look for an advisor with a fiduciary responsibility. A recent study by the Certified Financial Planner Board of Standards found that only about 20% of Americans work with a CFP® professional, meaning the vast majority rely on their own judgement or work with financial advisors who may not have a fiduciary obligation. While you may not need a financial advisor right now, understanding your risk comfort level is crucial.

EXTRA CREDIT: A fiduciary is a person that acts on behalf of another person, putting their clients' interests ahead of their own. A fiduciary has a legal and ethical duty to act in your best interest. Talk to friends, family, or even do an internet search, and see if you can find a financial planner with a fiduciary responsibility in your area. You may not need them now but it is good to know how to access resources when they are needed.

Ultimately the key to successful investing is finding the right balance between risk and reward that aligns with your goals and your risk tolerance. It is important to remember that just like leading a classroom, investments carry some degree of risk. The potential for higher returns often comes with a higher level of risk.

If you do not know where to start, or if you have already started and want to check to see whether your risk tolerance is acceptable I have two general tips for you.

- **The 120 Minus Age Rule:** Subtract your age from 120 and the result is the percentage of investments that should be in stocks. For a 25 year old just starting out their educational career, 120 - 25 = 95% of investments in stocks. The remaining portion would go into less risky assets, primarily bonds. This is of course a general rule. If your number seems too high or too low for your risk tolerance, adjust accordingly. Some experts recommend using 110 as the starting number instead. With that formula 110 - 25 = 85% would be the suggested percentage of investments in stocks. If you are a public school educator with a pension, I find the 110 formula to be too conservative. A pension provides a guaranteed monthly check in retirement for life, so I think you can afford to take slightly more risk with your investments. But that reflects my personal risk tolerance and yours may vary.

- **Target Date Funds:** You can invest in a target date retirement fund. Most investment plans offer them and they automatically become more conservative as you age, without any additional work on your part. More on this option later in the chapter.

Index Investing

Educators like clear step-by-step instructions. When I was an administrator working in a remote school where staff worked from home and went into the field to meet students one-on-one, no matter how clearly I wrote instructions or explained a process, revisions were always necessary to make the steps even clearer. You probably experience the same when working with students or staff.

Once you have an idea of your risk tolerance and how much of your investments you are comfortable allocating to stocks, the next step is to consider the types of investments to put your money into. Indexing is a passive investment strategy that seeks to replicate the performance of a market index, such as the S&P 500, by investing in a portfolio of securities that closely match the index. This approach aims to achieve returns similar to those of the index, rather than trying to outperform the market.

Think of an index fund as the school yearbook photo. Instead of hiring a professional photographer to take pictures one student at a time (active management), you take a picture of the entire student body (the market). You are guaranteed to capture the overall look and feel of the school, without the risk of a single photo being a complete failure and without the additional cost.

The most common way to invest in an index is through an index fund or an exchange-traded fund (ETF). These funds hold a diversified portfolio of stocks or other securities weighted according to their representation in the underlying index. For example, if a company represents 5% of the index, the fund will invest 5% of its assets in that company's stock.

Indexing offers several benefits to investors. First, it is a low-cost investment strategy because it does not require active management, which results in lower fees and expenses. Fund managers do less work which saves you money. Second, it provides broad market exposure, allowing investors to build a diversified portfolio of stocks or other securities. Finally, because it is a passive strategy, it may be less risky than actively managed strategies that attempt to beat the market. In general, actively managed funds do not consistently outperform passive options, so why pay more when you do not get more? Statistics from S&P and Dow Jones indexes consistently show that over a ten-year period, more than 85% of actively managed mutual funds fail to beat their benchmark index. Educators are smarter than that!

Any investing, including indexing, does not guarantee returns or protect against losses. Market volatility, changes in the composition of the underlying index, and other factors can affect the performance of an index fund or ETF. This is why we started with a discussion on risk tolerance. I am scaffolding the information.

Investment Choices

It is important to get student buy-in in your class. As students age and their independence grows, believing in what they are learning or in the way you are approaching it, it makes the process smoother for everyone involved. By this point in the book, I hope you are buying into the need to invest, the type of account you should be using, and why index investing is the best approach for the average middle-class educator.

You can invest in almost anything. That does not mean you should. Let us focus on three investment options you are most likely to encounter.

Mutual Funds

When it comes to your school sponsored investment program such as a 403b, you will likely have several mutual fund options to choose from. Mutual funds are not the same as index investing. However, index investing can be done through a mutual fund. This is similar to telling a student that a square is a rectangle but a rectangle is not always a square.

Mutual funds are managed investment portfolios that pool money from many investors to purchase securities such as stocks, bonds, and other assets.

Mutual funds can be actively managed, meaning a professional manager who is paid significantly more than you or I, decides which stocks are included in the fund. When you invest in a mutual fund, you are buying into all the stocks within that fund.

Mutual funds can also be passively managed, in which case the fund follows a specific index. A mutual fund can focus on many areas, but you should look for one that tracks a broad index. Common examples include large-cap companies, bonds, the total market etc.

Exchange Traded Funds (ETFs) and Stocks

In a Roth IRA, you typically have several investment options beyond mutual funds. Two of the most common are Exchange Traded Funds (ETFs) and individual stocks.

- **ETFs** are similar to mutual funds, but they trade on an exchange like individual stocks. Whereas mutual funds often allow investors to purchase partial shares, ETFs usually require you to buy a full share at the current market price.

- **Stocks**, on the other hand, represent ownership in a single company and are also bought and sold on an exchange. Investors must purchase whole shares rather than partial shares.

Mutual funds and ETFs are known for providing diversification within an investment portfolio. They invest in a variety of assets, which can include stocks, bonds, or other securities. This diversification spreads investment risk across many holdings, making these options generally less risky than investing in individual stocks.

Individual stocks are less diversified because they represent ownership in one company. They are considered to be riskier investments since a single company's value can rise or fall sharply based on factors such as company performance or overall economic conditions. For casual investors with limited capital, individual stocks are often best avoided. In many cases, popular stocks from large companies are already included in the mutual funds or ETFs you may be investing in.

Mistakes Help Us Grow: In my 20s I opened up a brokerage account so I could invest in the stock market with a small amount of "play" money. The first stock I bought was in a tech company my brother-in-law worked for that made biodiesel out of algae. That stock eventually became worthless and the company closed. I lost all my invested money and my brother-in-law did not get a Christmas present that year. The second stock I bought was Sprint, a telecommunications company. The stock proceeded to go on a slow decline until being purchased by another company. I got back less money than I put in. That was the end of my individual stock picking days.

However, as we discussed previously much of personal finance is behavioral. If you are like the kid sitting with their hand up in the air, waving it back and forth, knees bouncing at their desk because they are excited to ask a question, it may be better to set aside a small amount of your money to experiment with in the market. Choose an amount that will be inconsequential to your overall retirement plan, and pick a few stocks simply to learn and enjoy the process.

Mutual funds and ETFs charge fees to investors, which cover the cost of managing the portfolio. Mutual funds usually charge an expense ratio, which is a percentage of the total assets invested. ETFs charge similar expense ratios, but they are typically lower than those of mutual funds. Stocks do not charge fees beyond commissions paid to brokers when buying or selling. Depending on the brokerage you use, you may not pay any fees at all. Fees will be discussed in more detail in a later section as they are something you should always watch out for.

Mutual funds typically require a minimum investment, which can range from a few hundred to several thousand dollars. ETFs and stocks can be purchased in smaller dollar amounts, making them more accessible to newer investors, although they must be purchased as whole shares at the market price for that day.

Target-Date Funds

Age based mutual funds, also known as target-date funds, are a one-stop solution for investing. If investing is not something you feel comfortable with, this option is often the simplest choice for you. Also, kudos for pushing past your discomfort and making it this far in the book! Industry data shows that target-date funds are the default option for more than 75% of 403b and 401k plans today, making them easily accessible for most educators.

These funds are a type of mutual fund that automatically adjusts its asset allocation based on investor's age and time horizon. Working with students may keep you young at heart but time still moves forward. Target-date funds are designed to be a simple, all-in-one investment solution for retirement planning. If you invest $100 per year, the full amount goes into a single fund, which then allocates the money for you so you do not need to think about your asset allocation.

The target date in the fund's name refers to the year in which you plan to retire and is typically offered in five-year increments. For example, if you plan to retire in 2049, you may choose a target-date fund with a target year of 2050. As that target date approaches, the fund gradually shifts its investments from more aggressive, growth-oriented investments like stocks to more conservative, income-oriented investments like bonds and cash. This progression is known as the glide path and details about it can be found through the investment company offering the fund.

> **EXTRA CREDIT:** Look up the target-date funds for the year closest to when you want to retire, and compare the glide paths of the big three investment companies (Vanguard, Fidelity, Schwab). Are they different? Which one are you most comfortable with?

Age-based mutual funds can be a strong option for educators who want a hands-off approach to investing and who want to benefit from automatic rebalancing and allocation changes as they age. The glide path is your pre-planned, fully differentiated lesson plan for your investment portfolio. It handles the hard work of adjusting over time, ensuring your risk level remains appropriate for your age.

If you have a pension, consider the age at which you plan to take it and select your target date retirement fund accordingly. For example, you might plan to take your pension as soon as you are eligible but delay tapping into your investment accounts until later. This could be because you plan to work part-time or because your spouse will still be working. In this case you would want an age based fund that aligns with the year you plan to start withdrawing from your investment. Otherwise you risk your portfolio becoming too conservative too early, which may limit how much it earns through the stock market. Investing is like a middle school dance. It is a little awkward but you still want to get it right.

Fees

Now that we have covered the different types of accounts you may encounter, the order of investing, your comfort level with risk, and a few common investment strategies, you are ready to consider the most important topics in investing: fees.

There are many types of fees you may encounter when investing in various financial products. The two most common are:

- **Management fees:** These fees are charged by an investment manager or financial advisor for overseeing your investment portfolio. They are usually calculated as a percentage of the assets under management and can range from 0.0% to 2% or more.

- **Expense ratio:** These fees are charged by mutual funds, exchange-traded funds, and other investment vehicles to cover the cost of running the fund. Expense ratios include administrative costs, trading costs, and other operational expenses.

Fees are deducted from your investment returns. Even if your fund loses money, you still pay the fee. The lower the fee, the less you pay. Period.

To illustrate the impact of high fees, consider this example: An expense ratio of 1.0% compared to a low-cost ratio of 0.1% can cost an educator with a $250,000 portfolio nearly $50,000 over a 20-year career, assuming a 7% annual return. That is an entire year's salary for many teachers, lost to fees alone.

Major investment companies such as Vanguard, Fidelity, and Charles Schwab, offer a wide variety of high-quality funds with expense ratios below 0.1%. In today's investing environment there is little justification for high management or expense ratio fees beyond increasing profits for the company rather than you.

Other fees may also apply. If you are reviewing fees for an IRA, a taxable brokerage account, or a 529 plan, essentially any investment account where you have choices, and you see any of these additional fees, run away. Run like your students who want to be first in line for lunch.

- **Front-End Load:** This is a sales charge that investors pay when purchasing a mutual fund or other investment product. The front-end load is deducted from the initial investment and can range from 1% to 5% or more.

- **Back-End Load:** Also known as a contingent deferred sales charge (CDSC), this fee is charged when an investor sells an investment product before a specified period, usually five to seven years. The back-end load decreases over time and may be waived entirely if the investor holds the investment for a certain length of time

- **Transaction Fees:** These fees are charged when buying or selling stocks, bonds, or other securities. Transaction fees can vary widely depending on the broker and the type of security being traded.

- **Performance Fees:** These fees are charged by some investment managers or hedge funds as a percentage of profits earned above a certain threshold. Performance fees are intended to align the interests of the investor and the investment manager.

The investment company's website should display fund fees prominently on the fund's main page. If the fees are not clearly listed, each fund has a prospectus (try making that a vocab word for your students!) which you can download to find detailed information about fees and investment objectives.

Unfortunately, when it comes to a 403b or other school-sponsored investment account, you do not have the same flexibility in choosing a carrier as you do with an IRA or 529 plan. In some cases, especially at small private schools with fewer employees to distribute costs, investment options may carry higher fees.

I encountered this situation while working at a private school. To manage it, I maxed out my Roth IRA, which I held with a large investment company offering low fees. I then contributed only enough to the school's 403b to receive the employer match. After all, an employer match is free money, even if the account itself has higher fees.

Socially Responsible Funds

As an educator, I am going to assume that you care about society and want the best for the world. That is why I am including this section in the book. Socially responsible investing is not typically an Investing 101 topic; however, it introduces an ethical lens to the investing process and is worth discussing.

Socially responsible funds are investment funds that aim to generate financial returns while also promoting ethical or socially responsible goals. These funds are evaluated using environmental, social, and governance (ESG) principles. They screen out companies that do not meet those criteria. This approach allows you to put your money where your values are through your investing habits. As long as these funds meet the criteria already discussed in this chapter, such as index investing and low fees, here are several reasons for you to consider investing in them.

- **Alignment with your values:** Investing in socially responsible funds allows you to align your investments with your personal values and beliefs. By supporting companies that prioritize social responsibility, you are investing in businesses that aim to make a positive impact on society and the environment.

- **Positive Impact:** Socially responsible funds invest in companies that emphasize environmental sustainability, human rights, and corporate governance. As a result, these funds can positively impact society by supporting organizations committed to meaningful change. Investing this way is similar to having a classroom mission statement for your money; you are choosing to invest in companies whose core values align with your own.

- **Risk Mitigation:** Companies that prioritize social responsibility are often better prepared to manage risks related to environmental damage, social unrest, and regulatory compliance.

- **Long-term Performance:** Studies show that socially responsible funds can perform as well as, and sometimes better than, traditional investment funds over the long term. This is often because socially responsible companies tend to be well-managed and focused on sustainable growth. Recent data suggests that several ESG funds have outperformed their conventional counterparts over the past five years.

Your school sponsored 403b or 457 plan may not offer socially responsible investment options, as available funds are limited by the plan itself. However, a Roth IRA typically provides access to a much broader range of choices, especially if your account is held with one of the major brokerage firms such as Vanguard, Fidelity, or Charles Schwab. Searching for terms like "socially responsible" or "ESG" should generate a list of eligible funds.

From there review each fund's investment objectives, performance history, and fees. If a fund meets your expectations and supports long-term growth so you can enjoy a secure retirement, then you are well on your way to putting your money to work for both yourself and the world.

Finding a Deal: Spending with Intention

You are an essential part of society, shaping young minds and imparting valuable knowledge to the future generations. However, being an educator can often be challenging, both emotionally and financially. Research shows that about one in six teachers works a second job.

Fortunately, there are various types of discounts available to educators that can help you save money and ease some of the financial burdens you face. This chapter covers common deals and discounts educators have access to that the general public does not. Think of these discounts as the small amount of money you get back after spending, on average, over $600 of your own money on classroom supplies every single year. It is time to start reclaiming a little bit of that investment.

I encourage you to do a web search for "teacher discounts" and you will find many options that may help you save money that can be put toward better purposes.

Eligibility: Showing Your Credentials

Although deals often advertise themselves as being for "teachers," most K-12 educators usually qualify. This includes counselors, administrators, librarians, and support staff. In most instances showing your school staff ID is enough to qualify for the discount.

For some larger, company-wide discounts, especially those offered by major online retailers, you may need to go through a third-party verification service. Companies such as ID.me handle the process of confirming your employment status, often by requiring a recent pay stub or an official school email address. Once verified, you gain access to an entire portal of savings.

In a few cases, you may need to present your official state-issued teaching or administrative license. In these situations, private school educators may not qualify. I encountered this limitation several times early in my career as a private school educator when I tried to access deals available to my public school counterparts. Some discounts are also limited to members of unions or other professional organizations, such as the National Education Association (NEA) and the American Federation of Teachers (AFT).

EXTRA CREDIT: If you are part of a union, check to see what member benefits and discounts are included in your union membership. Union travel discounts can often offer high dollar savings.

The bottom line is that there is a long tradition of many segments of society offering discounts or special deals to educators. Every time I visit a museum I ask whether an educator discount is available. It never hurts to ask. The worst that can happen is that they say no. The best outcome is saving money while feeling appreciated for the important work you do.

Educator Expense Tax Deduction

This is one of the easiest ways to get money back for the crucial work you do as an educator. Currently K-12 educators can deduct up to $300 in unreimbursed expenses. This amount changes over time, so it is wise to do a quick web search to confirm whether the limit has increased since the writing of this book.

According to the IRS, qualified expenses include costs you pay for professional development courses, books, supplies, computer equipment, including related software and services, other equipment, and supplementary materials used in the classroom. When claiming this deduction be sure to keep your receipts. You must have documentation to support the claim. You will need to report these expenses on your tax return in order to receive the deduction.

If you do not spend the full amount, that is perfectly fine. You can claim whatever you spent during the calendar year. This deduction applies whether you take the standard deduction or itemized deductions on your taxes. If you are unsure which option applies to you, most educators take the standard deduction, unless they have a complicated tax situation. In fact, more than 90% of Americans take the standard deduction.

One of the biggest benefits of the Educator Expense Deduction is that it is an "above-the-line" deduction. This means it reduces your taxable income before the standard deduction is even applied, making it valuable for nearly everyone.

Educational and School Supply Discounts

Many educational companies and institutions offer discounts to teachers on a wide range of products and services. For example, Apple provides educational pricing on select products, which can result in significant savings. Microsoft also offers special discounts on software and hardware for educators. In many cases you can access the full Office suite for free or at a reduced cost using your school email.

Other retailers that are essential to the educator life offer year-round or seasonal discounts:

- **Craft and Hobby Stores:** Stores such as Michael's often provide 10% to 15% off total purchases, which is helpful when buying supplies for bulletin boards, art projects, or science fair materials.

- **Educational Supply Stores:** Lakeshore Learning typically offers a 15% discount to their rewards members.

- **Retailers:** Stores like Target and office supply retailers frequently run Back-to-School or Teacher Appreciation promotions, increasing discounts to 20% or more for a limited time.

I never purchase back-to-school supplies for my own children without using an educator discount or coupon. It never hurts to check online or ask in store to see if you can secure a discount.

Travel Discounts

Educators can also take advantage of various travel discounts to save money on vacations, weekend getaways, and work-related trips.

If you are traveling for work, many hotels offer a government rate on room prices. You can ask for this rate when booking or select it during online checkout. Public school employees qualify because they are considered government employees. These rates are often significantly lower than the standard prices, with average savings of 20% or more. Be sure to bring your staff ID in case the hotel asks for verification at check-in.

Another option to consider is student travel. For about 15 years of my education career I traveled for free or at a reduced cost by leading student travel tours. These opportunities took me to Europe, South America, and across the United States. While supervising students required constant responsibility and long hours, similar to serving as a chaperone on an extended field trip, the experience was incredibly rewarding. I enjoyed working with students and was able to visit places and participate in experiences I would not have accessed otherwise.

Without these programs, the estimated out-of-pocket cost for a 10-day trip to Europe can exceed $4,000. Through student travel programs, the cost is often nothing more than your time. Two of the largest companies offering these opportunities are EF Educational Tours and World Strides, though many other organizations exist. If you love to travel and want to do so on an educator's salary, these programs can provide meaningful opportunities during your summer break.

REAL TEACHER TALK

I'm retired but I do seasonal jobs with a local University and work with a student travel company to cover travel plans.

- Russell (30 years as an educator)

Entertainment Discounts

Educators can also enjoy discounts on entertainment and leisure activities. Museums and art galleries often offer free or discounted admission to teachers with valid identification. In cities with major cultural institutions, a teacher ID can grant free access to multiple venues, turning a $25 per person admission into a cost-free cultural day. Keep your staff ID in your wallet when traveling or going out. You never know when it might save you a little money.

In addition, educators can receive discounted access to theme parks such as Disney World and Universal Studios, often through union or professional organization memberships. Similar to travel discounts, these offers may only be available if you are a member of the organization. It is also worth checking with your local zoo, historical sites, and regional theaters. Some may have unpublished policies that offer educators a small reduction ticket prices. This is often part of the community's way of saying, "Thank you for what you do."

Restaurant Discounts

The most common time to find restaurant discounts is during Teacher Appreciation Week in May. These offers are usually easy to locate with a quick web search a week or two before the event. In the past, educators frequently received free items, but over time many of these offers have shifted to discounts instead. While free meals were once common, recent years have seen a move toward 15% to 20% discounts or complementary side items, which still provides some savings.

These discounts can be especially helpful when dining out with family or friends. Educators should also check locally owned restaurants. Their discounts may not be widely advertised, but supporting local businesses is worthwhile as they often give back to the community.

As with any discount, it is only beneficial if it applies to something you already planned to purchase. Spending more money just to receive a discount defeats the purpose of being financially savvy. However, if dining out once or twice a week is already part of your routine, taking advantage of educator discounts makes practical sense.

Bookstore Discounts

As an educator, I hope you enjoy visiting brick and mortar bookstores. While my family purchases many books online, bookstores remain important centers of learning and opportunity within our communities. We often stop in, especially at used bookstores, when we are out and about.

Many bookstores offer teacher discounts on books and educational materials. However, if you are building a classroom library, purchasing used books can be an even more cost-effective option. Half Price Books offers a year-round educator discount, typically around 10%, for those who sign up for their program. Some magazines also extend discounts to educators.

To maximize your savings, keep receipts from classroom related book purchases and include them in your year-end educator expenses tax deduction. This approach allows you to support local bookstores, reduce your spending, and receive a tax benefit.

Insurance Discounts

Auto insurance companies often provide professional group discounts to teachers and other public service employees. In most cases, submitting a copy of your teaching or administrative license is enough to qualify. Companies such as Geico, Liberty Mutual, and Farmers offer affinity discounts that may range from a modest 5%

to 15% off your premium simply for listing "educator" as your occupation.

Horace Mann is an insurance company that specializes in serving educators and offers discounts on auto, home, and life insurance policies. The company is built specifically for our profession and is always worth considering.

We have discussed insurance previously in this book. The best approach is to work with an insurance broker who can help you find the best deal for the coverage you need. If you are satisfied with your current insurance company and do not want to shop for other carriers, at minimum call your provider and ask whether they offer a professional educator discount.

Gym Memberships and Wellness Discounts

Several gym chains, including Fitness 19 and the YMCA have been known to offer discounts to educators, although availability varies by location. Time is the greatest resource we have. We trade the hours of our lives to work so we can earn money to survive, and hopefully one day have enough money to not have to work. Exercise plays an important role in protecting that time. Your health is a valuable asset that deserves attention and effort. In a profession known for high stress and burnout, prioritizing physical health is one of the smartest investments you can make in your career longevity.

That said, a gym membership is not required to be healthy. During the pandemic my gym closed and I transitioned to working out at home, which I continued for several years after the pandemic ended. There are countless free virtual workout classes available online. In addition, some of my previous employers offered free wellness classes, which provided a refreshing change from my usual routines. It is absolutely possible to build an effective wellness routine without a gym membership.

If you work in a middle or high school, you may also be able to use the school weight room. Check with your administration to see whether this is allowed. Whatever option you choose, do not neglect your health. If you do join a gym, ask what type of educator discount they offer.

Clothing Discounts

Many clothing retailers participate in educator discount programs. Discounts of 10% to 15% are common at popular stores such as J. Crew, Loft, Madewell, and Adidas. Your educator status typically must be verified through an external service such as ID.me, or by enrolling in the retailer's education program.

I have never personally taken advantage of these discounts. I prefer shopping at thrift stores, both for the lower cost and for the ethical benefits of reusing clothing and keeping items out of landfills. Thrifting does require patience and some digging, but that is part of the enjoyment. While I do not exclusively shop at thrift stores, I never pay full price when buying new clothing. Paying full price for clothes is unnecessary and a poor use of your hard-earned money.

If you have a favorite clothing brand, consider signing up for its e-newsletter so you can access sales that are often better than educators discounts. However, this only works if your spending habits are under control and your budget is balanced. If you are struggling to manage your budget, overwhelmed by debt, or unable to save and invest, you should not be purchasing new clothes regardless of the size of the discount. Sorry not sorry. Join me in the adventure of thrift store shopping as an easy and effective way to reduce spending.

Professional Development Discounts

In most cases, professional development (PD) should be provided by your school. Federal Title II funding is allocated to school districts to support teacher training. When I was an administrator I prioritized using PD funds to give teachers choice in how they met their yearly PD goals. Every educator has endured enough mandatory in-house sessions while wishing they could instead attend a conference or a training that aligned more closely with their interests.

The good news is that free professional development opportunities are widely available. Curriculum providers, educational technology companies, and community organizations frequently offer no-cost training led by experienced professionals.

Even better, some summer professional development programs will pay you to attend. I had a colleague who taught AP social studies courses and regularly found paid summer programs, many of which took place across the country. Other colleagues accessed paid opportunities through their school districts or state agencies, such as curriculum writing stipends or specialized summer institutes sponsored by universities or nonprofit organizations.

One university near where I previously lived in Wisconsin offers a free week-long summer institute held on a 400+ acre lakeside estate. Participants are not paid but room and board are covered and they spend a relaxing week learning alongside K-12 educators and college professors. Programs like this are not uncommon. Free opportunities for professional growth exist everywhere, but you have to seek them out. If you are unsure where to begin, ask colleagues at your school or educators who teach the same grade level or subject area.

Finally, if you are determined to attend a specific professional development conference that requires payment and your school will not cover the cost, check with your union or professional organization to see whether discounted registration is available. Another option is to apply as a breakout session presenter, since presenters receive reduced fees. This allows you to save money while sharing the great work you are already doing.

If you are early in your career, the idea of presenting at a conference may feel intimidating. That is completely normal. Give yourself time. If you are a veteran educator who has never presented to peers, I strongly encourage you to consider it when the opportunity arises. Presenting can be fun, energizing, and deeply rewarding. You may not feel like an expert, but if you identify something you care about and do well, chances are there are others who can benefit from your experience.

Conclusion

I hope this chapter has shown you that there are many opportunities to save some money on things you would normally spend on anyway. Keep your staff ID card with you, always ask if a teacher discount is available, and spend wisely. Beyond the examples listed in this chapter, saving money is a mindset and a habit. You know yourself best. Some of these areas may matter more to you than others. If that is the case, look for ways to cut spending in other areas. For instance, if you are a fashionista, thrift store shopping might not suit you. However, yard sales for furniture or discounts on meals and school supplies could save you money without crimping your style.

I love traveling but it is quite expensive so I have always found ways to make it work, such as traveling with students for free or at low cost. Now that I have children I cannot be gone for weeks at a time during the summer, so those types of travel experiences are on hold. That does not mean I will never be able to take advantage of them again. For now, we make sacrifices in other areas so we can have money for family vacations. They are not elaborate but we get to travel around the country while still staying within our budget, reflecting our financial priorities both now and for the future.

The same is true for you. Being financially responsible now gives you opportunities in the future, but you cannot set your future self up for failure through your spending habits today.

Fortunately, many companies and organizations recognize the value of your work and offer discounts to help you save money and reduce some of the financial burdens you face. Do not buy more than you need, but when you do make purchases, be sure to take advantage of your discounts.

Wallace

Teaching Financial Literacy: Extending the Lesson

O ver the many years it took me to write this book, between grading papers, avoiding computer work during the summer, and raising kids, personal finance has become an increasingly common subject taught in schools. A growing number of states now require personal finance as a graduation requirement. Given the staggering lack of financial understanding among so many in our society today, including within our own profession, helping high schoolers get a head start on managing money is not just a good idea; it is an urgent educational priority. The facts speak for themselves: on average, teachers earn only about 73 cents for every dollar earned by comparable college-educated professionals. When you consider the advanced degrees and certification requirements most of us have, that statistic hits you like a surprise administrative duty just before the bell rings.

My hope is that perhaps sometime in the future you are picking up an old, well-used copy of this book and thinking these words are outdated because personal finance has become a standard, universally mandated part of the curriculum across the country. Currently, however, despite the undeniable importance of financial stability, it is still not a universal part of the curriculum. In fact, while many of us entered education to solve other people's problems, we often neglect our own financial stability. A Stanford-led study revealed that nearly half of all teachers surveyed were frequently anxious about their finances, compared to only 17% of the general population. In another study 66% of teachers expressed interest in professional development about personal finance.

This book can help fill this knowledge gap. It provides the tools you need to make informed financial decisions for yourself while also empowering you to pass that crucial knowledge on to the next generation. The return on investment for teaching these skills is enormous, especially considering that teachers experiencing financial anxiety are 50% more likely to leave their jobs within two years, creating instability that hurts students and costs schools billions in turnover.

Teaching Foundational Financial Concepts

As you hopefully learned from this book, money management is about numbers, planning, and thinking through decisions. These are not abstract concepts; they are skills that can be taught to almost any grade in a developmentally appropriate way. Think of it as scaffolding: you would not teach an eighth-grader calculus, but you would teach them how to find the slope of a line, which is a foundational concept. Financial literacy works the same way.

The concept of delayed gratification and getting something of value by giving up something else are important ideas. In the classroom, we often teach this without realizing it. Many teachers use behavioral intervention plans where students earn tickets for appropriate behavior that they can trade in for a prize. The more tickets they have, the bigger the prize. You are essentially running a micro-economy, teaching the principles of saving (collecting more tickets) and compounding (the bigger prizes offer better value for more tickets) in a concrete, low-stakes environment.

As I mentioned previously, I used "oops passes" that students could use if they needed to go to the bathroom or get something from their locker during class. Unused oops passes could be redeemed for full credit on a homework assignment. It was amazing how many "I really have to use the bathroom" became "I can hold it" when asked for an oops pass. Indirectly, though they did not realize it, I was teaching them about the value of delayed gratification and encouraging cost-benefit analysis to determine how badly they wanted to leave class.

At a project-based-learning school where I worked, students had to complete a wellness project each year. We emphasized the wellness wheel and the seven dimensions of wellness: emotional, intellectual, physical, social, environmental, spiritual, and financial. We reinforced the power of early investing by posting bright green flyers around the school with facts such as "For every dollar an 18-year-old invests, it has the chance to turn into $100 by the time you retire." These were small reminders that decisions today can have a life-altering impact on the future. Think about your own real-life, sometimes painful experience with cost-benefit analysis: like more than 90% of teachers, you probably spend your own money on classroom supplies, averaging around $600 a year. Every time you buy that box of crayons or a ream of paper, you perform a financial analysis: the benefit of having the materials now outweighs the cost from your own budget. That is a lesson your students need to understand before it affects their own future.

Weaving Finance into the Curriculum

No matter the age or subject you teach, you have opportunities to introduce these principles. Financial literacy does not have to be a new elective course; it can be integrated into your existing curriculum, much like teaching critical thinking or digital citizenship.

For example, if I were teaching U.S. history, I likely would not have time, nor would it be appropriate, to spend a month covering personal finance. However, when discussing the Great Depression, I could incorporate a lesson on budgeting, debt, or the role of the Federal Reserve to connect real-world examples to the historical topic. If you are teaching English and assigning *A Raisin in the Sun*, that is a perfect opportunity to discuss generational wealth, budgeting, and financial risk. In a high school science class, when discussing half-life and decay, you can use an analogy about debt and interest rates and how they can either decay future stability or, in the case of compound interest, exponentially grow wealth.

If I were teaching second grade and following Common Core standards, counting money would already be part of the math curriculum. This could naturally extend to concepts such as needs versus wants or using a classroom economy to practice making choices with limited resources.

As an educator, you probably know that there are more resources available than you could ever incorporate into your lessons. The websites listed in the following pages are a great starting point. Some of them even include curated lists of additional websites offering more financial literacy resources. You are likely to find something suitable for the grade level you are teaching, Since these are websites, they can be updated regularly, unlike this book. Books, however, are still valuable and worth supporting!

Free Resources for Educators

Everything I mention in this chapter provides free resources. What kind of personal finance book for educators would this be if at the end it asked you to spend more money? Many of us know that low compensation is a major source of job dissatisfaction, with only 15% of teachers reporting they are very or extremely satisfied with their pay. The last thing you need is another required purchase.

My first suggestion is **Next Gen Personal Finance**, a non-profit organization that offers both curriculum and professional development for teachers. Their curriculum is designed for middle school and high school students. Many of the other websites link to this source, which is a strong indicator of its quality. Concepts are organized by units or you can access a full semester or year-long course. There are even online games for students to play. You can explore their comprehensive website at https://www.ngpf.org/.

The **Federal Reserve Bank** provides a free full-curriculum they created, with resources for all grade levels. You can find their main education page at https://www.federalreserveeducation.org/. Their program can sync with many popular LMSs. Using these resources provides a bonus opportunity to teach your students about the role of the Fed in our country's money supply. Maybe you too need to learn what the Fed does, and that is okay.

My Classroom Economy is a personal finance curriculum resource for all grade levels. It is created and maintained by Vanguard. You can access it at https://myclassroomeconomy.org. In My Classroom Economy, students earn and spend money in a simulated microeconomy. For example, they pay "rent" for their desks and it is designed to overlay, not replace, your regular general education curriculum. Everything you need from detailed instructions to handouts is included.

Practical Money Skills is a clearinghouse of sorts for financial literacy. There are professional development training sessions for you, lessons for your students, and even some interactive games. They partnered with the NFL and FIFA to create a Financial Football Game and a Financial Soccer game for students. You can find out more at https://www.practicalmoneyskills.com/.

Hands on Banking is an award-winning financial education program available in English and Spanish. It offers non-commercial content such as lesson plans, instructor guides, courses, activities and more. Their website: https://youth.handsonbanking.org/.

Rich Kid Smart Kid offers online games that teach personal finance skills for elementary students. You know how much your students like to play online games. Find the games at www.richkidsmartkid.com.

Of course, all of the major curriculum publishers now offer personal finance programs. If you are fortunate enough to work for a school system that supports a personal finance class and is willing to purchase one of these programs, that is excellent. However, if that is not the case, there is no need to spend your hard-earned money on a curriculum when so many high-quality resources are available for free. It is simply a matter of having the time and energy to integrate them into your existing lessons.

A Message for School Leadership

If you support the idea but are unsure how or when to start, consider April which is Personal Finance Month. Even if you cannot incorporate personal finance principles throughout the entire year, April is a perfect opportunity to conduct a unit on the topic. There are many finance games available that you can play with your students. Choose one or two activities and find a way to incorporate them into your students' learning.

If you are an administrator reading this, consider organizing a professional development session on incorporating personal finance into the classroom. This is not just a compliance requirement or a nice-to-have initiative; it is a critical tool for retaining staff and stabilizing your school community. With more than four in ten teachers reporting burn out, schools face a significant well-being challenge. Because financial stress is a major contributor to this burnout and is directly linked to teacher turnover, providing training and resources is an investment in your people. Empower teachers to select one of the free resources above that they feel will work best for their students. Allow them to brainstorm ideas, as teachers know their students best. Trust their judgment in a low-stakes situation like adding a supplementary concept such as personal finance.

You could also plan a school-wide initiative in April. Announce it in the newsletter, invite a financial professional to speak for career day, and invite parents to discuss money at home. There are many steps administrators can take to promote financial literacy, regardless of the type of school you lead. Yes, your workload is heavy, and like teachers, administrators face challenges when adding new initiatives. However, with so few schools genuinely supporting financial literacy, you have an opportunity to innovate and add meaningful, measurable value to your student's education. You are not just creating knowledgeable students; you are helping to build resilient future citizens.

Wallace

The Final Lesson: Designing Your Financial Future

$

You made it. You closed the textbook, finished the final unit, and are now packing up your mental whiteboard. If this book were a semester-long course, you have just turned in the final, and congratulations, you earned an A.

I know reading a personal finance book was probably the last thing you wanted to do, wedged somewhere between grading papers and avoiding emails from parents. But you did it. You pushed through the jargon, figured out the PEMDAS of investing, and faced the uncomfortable reality that while education is an intrinsically noble profession, you do not have to be a financially martyred one.

The truth is, we are excellent planners. We can map out a year's worth of curriculum, differentiate a lesson for different learning groups, and write detailed behavioral intervention plans that account for every possible scenario. The irony is that we often stop planning when we look at our own paycheck. We are great at helping students see the long-term implications of their choices, but we struggle to apply that same vision to high-fee mutual funds or unaddressed debt.

Your Long-Term Project

Remember how we discussed that the first, most important step is often the simplest? It is the financial equivalent of scaffolding a lesson. You needed to get the easy, guaranteed wins first:

- The Power of the Match: For public school employees, your pension is your match. For private school employees, hitting that employer match is an automatic return on your retirement account investment before any market gains.

- The Roth IRA's Flexibility: You learned that your Roth IRA offers tax-free growth and the flexibility to withdraw contributions if life throws an unexpected emergency your way. Since you will have an emergency fund, you should not need to tap your Roth IRA and can instead let it grow until retirement.

- The Low-Fee Strategy: You saw that seemingly small expense ratios are like tiny points deducted every day. Over a 30-year career, a 1% fee difference can cost as much as a new car, or perhaps the ability to retire one year earlier.

You did not just read about delayed gratification; you put it into practice by hopefully setting up automatic investments. You learned that financial freedom is not a sudden win, but rather the cumulative effect of hundreds of small, correct daily decisions. It is like a successful school year, not defined by one amazing field trip, but by the relentless, quiet commitment to showing up and doing the work day after day.

REAL TEACHER TALK

Start a retirement account on day one.

- Amy (29 years as an educator)

Financial Health for Professional Health

And that brings us to the final lesson: the connection between your financial health and your professional mission.

When you are constantly stressed about money, when you are part of the four-out-of-ten teachers reporting chronic burnout, that anxiety becomes contagious. Studies show that a teacher's high stress levels can actually elevate stress hormones in their students.

But the future can be different. You have a plan. You have systems in place. You have a sense of control over your financial destiny. This stability gives you the bandwidth to be the best professional you want to be. It allows you to be the educator who:

- Stays because you want to, not because you are desperately chasing a slightly higher salary down the road.

- Does not internalize the sting of a low salary because you know your money is working as hard as you are

- Leans into teaching financial literacy because you know the material firsthand.

You are now a walking, talking example of your best lesson. When you teach a student about cost-benefit analysis, you can ground it in your own experience, even if you never explicitly mention your Roth IRA balance. When you show them that one dollar invested at age 18 can turn into $100, you are teaching them the most powerful principle of all: time is your greatest asset.

The Retirement P.D.

We all love the moment on the last day of school when you lock your classroom door and know you have done your best. You walk away, but the impact of your work does not. That is the real pension of teaching: the human capital you have built, the minds shaped, the quiet, and life-altering lessons that continue to compound years after the student has left your class.

Your personal finance journey is no different. You have put in the work, established the foundations, and automated the process. Now, let time and compound interest take over.

Your financial house is in order. You have written your own successful financial curriculum, and in 20 or 30 years, you will receive the biggest paycheck of all: a financially free retirement, paid for by the wise choices you started making today.

That is the kind of long-term assignment you will never regret grading.

Appendix A: Educator Side Hustle Directory

W e established that your salary is the starting point, but it should not be the finish line. Since adding extra hours to your day is impossible and negotiating a higher salary is often futile, the most practical financial move is generating supplementary income.

This is a basic directory of ways educators can earn more. I have divided it into two categories: High-Leverage Skills (using your teaching expertise for maximum value) and Flexible Hourly Work (for when you just need consistent, guaranteed cash flow). As you will see in the "Real Teacher Talk" section at the bottom of this appendix, there is no limit to the type of side hustle you can pursue.

Category 1: High-Leverage Skills

Focus on options that leverage your professional knowledge, as these will yield the highest return for your time and minimize the burnout associated with low-wage gigs.

- **Specialized Test Prep Tutoring:** Offer one-on-one or small group tutoring for high-stakes exams (SAT/ACT, AP courses, GRE, GMAT, professional licensing, or Praxis tests for new teachers). Use your content mastery, data analysis, and pacing skills to deliver results.

- **Curriculum Creation & Sales:** Develop and sell high-quality, pre-made resources (lessons, complete units, specialized rubrics, digital escape rooms, interactive Google Slides, differentiated bundles) on platforms like Teachers Pay Teachers. This monetizes the lesson design and alignment work you already do.

- **Online Adjunct/Continuing Education Instruction:** Teach a single college-level course (requires a Master's) or develop and teach Continuing Education units for adults (e.g., teaching Excel, professional writing, advanced presentation skills). This leverages your advanced content knowledge and adult learning principles.

- **Curriculum Consulting/Editing:** Take on contract work for textbook publishers, Ed-Tech companies, or assessment firms to write, review, or align instructional materials with standards. This may include sensitivity reading or bias review, utilizing your attention to detail and professional writing skills.

- **Academic Coaching/IEP Consulting:** Support students needing help with organization, time management, or study skills. Sell your expertise to parents navigating the IEP/504 process as an independent advocate.

- **Teacher Professional Development (PD):** Design and lead workshops for other schools or conferences on specialized topics (e.g., using AI in the classroom, restorative justice, advanced data analysis). This utilizes your public speaking and specialized teaching methods.

- **Educational Video Creation:** Start a YouTube channel or TikTok channel to break down complex homework problems, offer study tips, or create short educational animations. Monetize through platform ads, sponsorships, or Patreon.

- **Technical Writing/Grant Writing:** Apply your writing and organizational skills to create technical documentation for local companies or draft grant proposals for non-profits.

Category 2: Flexible Hourly Work

These options may not require a teaching degree, but they provide predictable wages and are ideal for summer breaks or for teachers who want to separate their side hustle from their main job.

- **Hospitality/Service Industry:** Work the peak tipping shifts for maximum cash flow. Examples include fine dining server, catering hall bartender, movie theater employee on busy nights, or stadium concessions lead during games.

- **Testing/Proctoring/Exam Centers:** Administer college entrance exams (SAT, ACT, etc.) or professional certification exams for testing companies or universities. This work is sporadic but utilizes reliability and professionalism.

- **Niche Summer Labor/Seasonal Work:** Take temporary summer work in high-demand fields. Examples include managing public pools, leading painting crews, serving as a summer camp administrative director, or working as a museum guide/docent.

- **Personal Services/Organization:** Provide reliable, skilled services for busy professionals. Examples include home organizing, personalized concierge services (e.g., scheduling, managing home repairs), pet sitting/dog walking, or house sitting for long-term travelers.

- **Administrative/Virtual Assistant:** Contract work supporting small businesses with administrative tasks, data entry, customer scheduling, or managing social media accounts and email funnels. This work is remote and flexible in the evenings.

- **Retail/Specialty Sales:** Work in boutique or specialty stores that offer commission or offer staff discounts. Examples include bookstores, outdoor gear shops, or clothing boutiques.

- **Logistics/E-Commerce Support:** Drive for a food delivery or rideshare company, or assist small e-commerce businesses with packaging and shipping. These roles are extremely flexible and can be done during peak hours.

Critical Financial Reminder for 1099 Income

If you pursue independent contractor work such as tutoring, curriculum creation, or consulting, you will receive a 1099 form instead of a W-2. You are responsible for setting aside money for taxes yourself. Do not wait until April 15th. Set aside 25% of every payment and place it into a separate, high-yield savings account to cover your quarterly estimated taxes. This is a non-negotiable financial rule for self-employment.

REAL TEACHER TALK: The educators who provided feedback on this book reported having done the following side-gigs at some point in their careers:

Swim instructor, lifeguarding, tutoring, coaching, refereeing, adjunct college instructor in the evenings, overtime hours offered through my district, substituting during prep periods, summer school teaching, teaching online for another school, singing and performing music, waitressing, starting my own small business helping families homeschool, Zamboni driver, stadium manager, golf course ranger, therapeutic support staffer, supervising credential candidates, being a paid mentor for new teachers, scoring professional exams for Pearson, consulting, camp counselor/director, seasonal retail worker, Fish and Game boat safety officer, tire tech, being a public speaker, radio announcer, managing my investment properties

Appendix B: Sample Line Item Budget

INCOME SOURCES	NET INCOME	EXPENSES	BUDGET
My Income		Mortgage	
Spouse Income		Utilities	
Side Hustle Income		House Maintenance	
Rental Income		Yard	
Interest		Cell Phone	
Other		Groceries	
TOTAL INCOME	**$ X,XXX**	Restaurants	
		Alcohol	
SAVINGS RATE	**XX %**	Household goods	
		Miscellaneous shopping	
To calculate savings rate:		Education	
(net income - spending) /	net income x 100	Pets	
		Clothing	
		Grooming	
		Charity	
		Health/Medical	
		Gym Membership	
		Kids Activities	
		Media	
		Entertainment	
		Gifts	
		Vacation	
		Car Loan	
		Gas/Parking	
		Car Maintenance	
		Car Registration	
		Car Insurance	
		Life Insurance	
		TOTAL SPENDING	**$ X,XXX**

REAL TEACHER TALK

Frugality and living minimally is often just as powerful a financial security as building a big retirement fund.

- Jason (17 years as an educator)

Appendix C: State Teacher Pension System Links

Y our pension is a critical part of your financial plan, but every state calls it something different (TRS, PERS, SERS, etc.). More importantly, every state has different vesting requirements and rules for moving or withdrawing funds. If you ever plan to teach in a different state, or if you simply need to find the definitive source for your own benefits, use this directory. I recommend bookmarking your state's link.

Note: While these links were active at time of publication, state governments occasionally update their domains. Search for your state's "Teacher Retirement System" if a link does not work.

Alabama - https://www.rsa-al.gov/index.php/trs/

Alaska - https://drb.alaska.gov/employee/dbrplan.html

Arizona - https://www.azasrs.gov/

California - https://www.calstrs.com/

Colorado - https://www.copera.org/

Connecticut - https://portal.ct.gov/trb

Delaware - https://www.delawarepensions.com/

District of Columbia - https://dcrb.dc.gov/

Florida - https://www.myfrs.com/

Georgia - https://www.trsga.com/

Hawaii - https://ers.ehawaii.gov/

Idaho - https://www.persi.idaho.gov/

Illinois - https://www.trsil.org/

Indiana - https://www.in.gov/inprs/

Iowa - https://www.ipers.org/

Kansas - https://www.kpers.org/

Kentucky - https://trs.ky.gov/

Louisiana - https://www.trsl.org/

Maine - https://www.mainepers.org/

Maryland - https://www.sra.state.md.us/

Massachusetts - https://mtrs.state.ma.us/

Michigan - https://www.michigan.gov/ors/

Minnesota - https://www.minnesotatra.org/

Mississippi - https://www.pers.ms.gov/

Missouri - https://www.psrs-peers.org/

Montana - https://trs.mt.gov/

Nebraska - https://npers.ne.gov/

Nevada - https://www.nvpers.org/

New Hampshire - https://www.nhrs.org/

New Jersey - https://www.nj.gov/treasury/pensions/

New Mexico - https://www.erb.nm.gov/

New York - https://www.nystrs.org/

North Carolina - https://www.myncretirement.gov/

North Dakota - https://www.rio.nd.gov/tffr-member

Ohio - https://www.strsoh.org/

Oklahoma - https://www.ok.gov/TRS/

Oregon - https://www.oregon.gov/pers/

Pennsylvania - https://www.pa.gov/agencies/psers

Puerto Rico - https://www.retiro.pr.gov/

Rhode Island - https://www.ersri.org/

South Carolina - https://www.peba.sc.gov/scrs

South Dakota - https://www.sd.gov/sdrs

Tennessee - https://treasury.tn.gov/tcrs

Texas - https://www.trs.texas.gov/

Utah - https://www.urs.org/

Vermont - https://www.vermonttreasurer.gov/vstrs

Virginia - https://www.varetire.org/

Washington - https://www.drs.wa.gov/

West Virginia - https://www.wvretirement.com/TRS.html

Wisconsin - https://etf.wi.gov/

Wyoming - https://retirement.wyo.gov/

Wallace

About the Author

Dr. Burke Wallace is a scholar-practitioner who has spent more than two decades navigating the complexities of the education system. Since beginning his career in 2004, he has served at nearly every level of the field— from classroom teacher and coach, to site-level and district-level administrator, to college professor.

Dr. Wallace's unique perspective on personal finance is fueled by his diverse academic background. He holds a Ph.D. in Leadership and an MBA, alongside master's degrees in Education and Religion. This rare combination of leadership, business, and pedagogical expertise allows him to bridge the gap between financial theory and the lived reality of school life.

Dr. Wallace holds teaching and administrative licensure in both California and Montana. He is married and has three adopted children.

www.ingramcontent.com/pod-product-compliance
Lightning Source LLC
Chambersburg PA
CBHW051419090426
42737CB00014B/2750